Praise for Peering T

"Peering Through the Veil is a comprehensive, enjoyable and enlightening book gifting the reader powerful insights, knowledge, and keys on meditation. Written in Takara's unique and friendly style, it inspires participation, compelling us to release old mindsets so we can enter the magical inner world she eludes to. This book is a must read for everyone ready to take their life to a deeper level and release the veils clouding their True Nature. Following Takara's gentle guidance and inspired exercises, we can return to the innocence, childlike wonder, and inner peace of our Authentic Self." - *Aurora Juliana Ariel, Ph.D., #1 Bestselling Author, Creator of TheQuest, and Award Winning Author of the Earth 2012 series*

"To even try to come up with words about Takara's totally comprehensive book about meditation wouldn't begin to give the potential reader an idea of the level of complexity and scope the book offers for finding "inner peace". The unique gift Takara has to bring the complex, complicated and much misunderstood topic of meditation and transforming it to simple understandable language with her gift of simplifying the mystical practice, benefits of meditation is remarkable. Not only that - she gives detailed instructions on the "how to" of various forms of meditation in order for you, the reader, to tailor and create any program for you as an individual. She does it marvelously with her superb story-telling abilities, deep, deep research, and a warrior's approach to "ferret" out the truth. This book is a rare find." - *Drs. Loren and Diane Mickelson*

"Not only did I get to read a highly entertaining story of Takara's spiritual adventures, but all these stories led to excellent advice and instructions regarding a multitude of ancient meditation tools. I found the story of how she found these techniques just as enlightening as the technical information she offers. I highly recommend this book!" - *Virginia Bonta Brown, Occupational Therapist, President, BioElectric Shield Co.*

"Takara has produced a readable, comprehensive guide on meditation, describing the phenomenal benefits that can be derived from such a practice. Her description of her personal journey is one that many can relate to and will provide support and inspiration for anyone who finds themselves evolving spiritually. This book will serve you in many ways. I highly recommend it!" – *Dr. Steven Farmer, best-selling author of Animal Spirit Guides, Earth Magic, and Earth Magic Oracle Cards. www.EarthMagic.net*

"This book is super comprehensive and covers a multitude of meditation techniques and ideas, interspersed with Takara's keen sense of storytelling to emphasize what she is describing. She has a great ability to keep the subject dynamic and interesting. It is also a great reference book, jam-packed with valuable information." – *Star Riparetti, Award Winning Author of Bliss and Blessings and Creator of Star Flower and Gemstone Essences*

"I have just finished reading Takara's beautiful book 'Peering through the Veil' and I have to say it is excellent. Simple, clear and very powerful. I commend her on the book. It will certainly be a useful 'guide' for people who are just awakening and those who have been awakened for some time and need a 'different' perspective on aspects of their lives and their practices. I found her writing style clear and easy to understanding. I recommend it highly !!!" - *David J. Adams, Australia*

"Peering Through the Veil is amazing!!! I loved it and learned so much. It actually felt as though Takara and I were just talking as she was explaining everything to me. The flow was conversational and the concepts were clear. I am new to meditation, so it was the perfect book at the perfect time...funny how the universe works! Thank you, Takara, for sharing this information!!!! Many people will be moved forward by this book." - *Misty Gregg, Preventative Healthcare Consultant and Owner, The Sage Soapbox*

Peering
Through the Veil

Also by Takara

7 Secrets:
To Dancing Through Life EmPOWERed, EnRICHed, and EnJOY!

Dancing with Dolphins:
Embracing Their Joy

Dolphins & Whales Forever *(#1 bestseller)*

Dowsing for Divine Direction
*Fine Tune Your Intuition While Improving
Every Area of Life*

The Dancing Dolphin Way Self Help Companion Tool:
Your Ultimate Guide to Wellbeing

**Life Works When You Are Happy, It Sucks When You
Are Not**

Manifesting Your Beloved:
Having a Love Relationship in Joy (out of print)

**Visit my website to get a free ebook– the *7 Secrets*
to Dancing Through Life EmPOWERed, EnRICHed, and
Living in JOY!** *(plus several other gifts!)*
https://www.MagnificentU.com/gift/

Peering

Through the Veil

The Simple Step-by-Step Guide to Meditation and Inner Peace

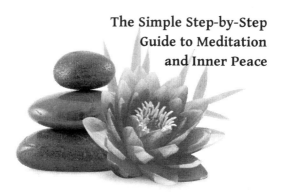

Debbie Takara Shelor

Forchianna Publishing
Radford, Virginia

Forchianna Publishing
P.O. Box 1363
Radford, VA 24143

Forchianna Publishing is a division of Forchianna L.L.C.

ISBN-10 1463560206
ISBN-13 978-1463560201

10 9 8 7 6 5 4 3 2 1

This book was typeset in Gentium Book Basic with Chopin Script used as display typeface

New Chapter Image – Zen Pebbles and Water Lilly by Beboy Ltd

Table of Contents

Foreword

Time seems to be speeding up and life going faster and faster. There's an acceleration that is occurring (or that most of us are experiencing) that allows for less time to do the things we enjoy and more time devoted to activities that demand our attention in order to simply survive. We're able to get fewer and fewer things accomplished in a day. For many, life seems a blur, with our attention focused on a seemingly never-ending process of activity that keeps us from doing what really matters and from being who we really are. We become stressed out and anxious and more.

But what if we could find a tool that was so simple; yet so effective that it could help us not only cope with this crazy world but could also bring us peace and tranquility? Takara has found this tool—the power of meditation, and shares this extraordinary gift with us through *Peering Through the Veil*. We have, right at our fingertips, an exceptional book that will assist each of us in discovering the joys of inner peace, and help us unlock the mysteries of discovering our authentic creativity and finding our inner truth.

Science is now validating what the ancient sages and mystics have known for many a millennium—that meditation can put us in touch with not only deeper aspects of self, but assist in creating harmony and balance for us on a physical, emotional, mental and spiritual level, and what a blessing this is, for it helps us lead healthier, happier lives.

Meditation is becoming more and more mainstream in our current culture. People want to know more about it and how they can personally benefit from it. I'm finding that so many of us are searching for guidance and tools to help us make sense out of the chaos and confusion that is often streaming around us. In *Peering Through the Veil*, Takara has brought forth this timely subject in what I consider to be an exceptional learning tool for people to experience the benefits of meditation within their own body/mind/spirit as she lays out a beautiful step-by-step process that is both easy to utilize and effective and actually fun!

In *Peering through the Veil*, Takara shares her own unique story about her introduction and journey into the world of meditation. We discover how this world changed her life and how it can change ours. Takara takes us on her personal journey that is both fascinating and insightful. In addition, she explores many different aspects of meditation, from different sounds, smells, spaces, and postures that can aid the meditation experiences to various brainwave states associated with different states of consciousness.

For myself, meditation has always been a powerful and essential tool to integrate into my life. Since my early twenties (almost 40 years ago!), I have been involved in the world of healing and spirituality—helping others along their journey as a teacher, licensed psychotherapist, astrologist, sound healer, author and — in all of these arenas I have incorporated meditation. I have studied many modalities of healing and transformation throughout the years and I know from a deep level how important and beneficial meditation is to achieve wellness.

I have had the honor and privilege of knowing my colleague and dear friend, Takara, and her work for many years. Knowing the depth and breadth to which she devotes her focus and time to all her spiritual endeavors and practices, it is my great joy to have been given this beautiful opportunity to contribute to such an exceptional and inspiring book. Her experience with meditation and her knowledge of this subject is a perfect recipe for anyone wishing to discover the joys of how it can enhance their life.

In this new and updated edition of *Peering Through the Veil*, the reader will find not only more inspirational life experiences shared by Takara as she weaves forth spiritual alchemy throughout, but will also be able to go into a deeper knowing of their own inner truth. It is said that a true teacher of meditation can transmit the essence of meditation simply through being in their presence. So it is with *Peering Through the Veil*. It's easy to feel a state of inner calm, openness, and joy, through which the subject of meditation is presented in this skillfully, delightfully, and brilliantly written book. I know you will enjoy this timely and important gateway into the world of meditation. Peace be with you.

Andi Goldman
Author, Chakra Frequencies
Visionary Award Winner

Notes About The Updated Edition

A great deal can change in 17 years. When the original version of *Peering Through the Veil* was first published as a PDF eBook in 2001, I had been enjoying meditation for 7 years. I was married, my son, Jess, was just a toddler, and New Mexico had been my home for only a brief time.

My son is now in college. I'm divorced. And after living in New Mexico for 9 magnificent years, I moved to the beautiful Blue Ridge Mountains of Virginia. I believe my writing ability has matured significantly.

They say it takes 10 years, 10,000 hours, or 10,000 times for a person to truly know, or master, anything.

I don't believe that meditation is something one ever truly masters. It is, however, something that I know very well having practiced it daily for the past 25 years. The longer you do it, the more profound the impact is in your life. It is a practice with exponentially increasing benefits.

In 2011, I received an email indicating that my original ebook (PDF) version of *Peering Through the Veil* had received an award as one of the top 50 eBooks about Positive Thinking and Visualization.

I was shocked.

First of all, it had been written 10 years prior to receiving the award. Second, I couldn't figure out how on earth anyone had even found it. It was buried deep within one of my websites and it wasn't something I actively promoted.

Few people had ever seen it.

I've been leading a spiritually-guided life long enough to know that nothing happens by chance. Every conversation, event, and person I encounter always has deeper meaning and significance. As soon as I got the email, I knew the Universe wanted me to do something more with the information in *Peering Through the Veil.*

The original PDF version contained the basic techniques for a few different forms of meditation. In the much-expanded first edition of the printed version, I added many more.

I also added several of my personal stories, visions, and highly esoteric / metaphysical meditation experiences that were not part of the original text. With all the stories added, I was jokingly tempted to change the name to "Takara's Adventures in Meditationland."

In addition to significantly more words, the printed version contained a guided meditation in MP3 format for readers to download.

I've grown older, wiser, and more enlightened over the many years since the original version first came out. My daily practice of deep meditation continues. I've experienced a seemingly endless number of Divinely-inspired meditations and moments, participated in and led many group guided meditations, and had numerous extraordinary spiritual experiences since then.

On several occasions, I've had the privilege of being asked to guide children through meditational journeys. It brings me great joy to do so as they take to it so readily.

Living in New Mexico, I had the opportunity of really getting to know, observe, and experience the Native American culture. And I was deeply blessed to have private audiences with "wise ones" from all over the world who came to participate in, or lead, ceremonies, workshops, and gatherings at The Spirit of Nature Retreat which I owned, managed, and facilitated many workshops through.

Several travel experiences turned into spiritual pilgrimages in which I grew in both wisdom and consciousness. A few of those include a trip to Mt. Shasta in California; swimming with wild dolphins in Bimini; several visits to Sedona, Arizona; an 8-day

Warriors in the Mist training with Stuart Wilde; living aboard a million-dollar yacht in Fiji and the South Pacific; and a writer's sabbatical near Taos, New Mexico where I stayed in a meditational trance for several days and "brought in" a whole new healing technology to heal the trauma drama of the past and become more centered, balanced, and at peace.

As I was writing my book on dowsing and describing how using a pendulum alters a person's brainwave state, I realized that dowsing can also be considered a powerful form of meditation if done in the way that I teach it.

In this update, I've added a fabulous new book cover as well as some much needed changes and clarifications in the text. Also in this update, I changed the font size to a slightly larger one. As I've gotten older, smaller fonts have become harder to read. I trust my older readers will appreciate this change.

There is now an optional powerful guided meditation audio program for those who wish to dive deeper after they have finished the book.

I trust that this new version of *Peering Through the Veil* will help you to enjoy and benefit from meditation as much as I and so many others have.

Takara

May 12, 2018

Dedication & Acknowledgements

Dedication

This book is dedicated to my dear friend, Karen Schweitzer, whose wise counsel and healing techniques helped me through one of the most difficult times of my life. I learned to meditate at her suggestion. Had I not gone down that road, this book, as well as many others, might not exist.

Acknowledgements

Thanks to these individuals and organizations, I have had the blessing of experiencing the various meditations and healing techniques described in this book:

- ❖ Stuart Wilde's books, meditations, audios, and the 8-day *Warriors in the Mist* experience
- ❖ Karen Schweitzer, whose advice, energetic healing methods, and support got me through a tsunami of change and who first encouraged me to learn to meditate
- ❖ Jonathan Goldman, Sound Healing Pioneer and a dear friend, for helping me to understand the power of sound for meditation and healing; and for his collaboration on the *Essences of Sound* product line, and the *Divine Name Workshops* that I have attended on many occasions.
- ❖ Greg Schweitzer and the *Body Mind Meditation*
- ❖ Jose Silva, Jeanie Bingston, and *The Silva Method*™
- ❖ 9-Month *Women's Wisdom* Course with Sue King, Hemitra Crecraft, and *Heart of the Goddess* which

included many shamanic journeys and introduced me to numerous energy healing modalities

❖ Neil Douglas Klotz, *Dances of Universal Peace*, and the *Desert Wisdom Weekend*

❖ Kaaren Shikiah Kaylor for helping me enter the Halls of Amenti and for bringing in the beautiful *Dancing Dolphin Healing Cards*

❖ Rebirthing with the *Alivening Weekend* by Glenn Smyly

❖ The numerous indigenous elders and shamanic teachers I've had the privilege of knowing

❖ Sun Bear, Wabun Wind and their book, *Dancing with the Wheel*, for the powerful meditation experience that literally changed my life

❖ Joseph Rael, known as Beautiful Painted Arrow, for teaching so many people about sweatlodge, sun moon dance, the power of sound and vibration, and his incredible global sound healing chambers

❖ Anne Hughes, whose teachings and Presence have had a monumental impact on my life and teachings

❖ Walt Woods, former head of the *American Society of Dowsers*, who showed me scientific proof of the changes in brainwaves as a person dowses

❖ Marsha Scarbrough, David Jonas, and others for their editorial assistance. Their insights and suggestions greatly improved the text.

❖ And finally, Millie Stefani, my dear friend, mentor, & Sister of the Heart, who for many years has meditated and dowsed with me practically every day.

Special thanks to my family and friends whose love, acceptance, encouragement, and support make it possible to bring forth books such as this: David J. Adams, Heather Browne, Donna Brownell, Katherine & James Burk, Dennis Culhane, Kat Cunningham, Julie Davis, Therese Francis, Andi & Jonathan Goldman, Roberta Goodman, Kaya Green, Misty Gregg, Jess Hicks,

David Jonas, Mark Joyner, Cyndie Lepori, Don McInnes, Diane & Loren Mickelson, AnnaMariah Nau, Jude Pardee, Cat Parenti & Grandma Chandra, Kathie Redmond, Laurie Reyon, Jake Rogers, Tammie Saver-Wolf, Tina Salazar, Thelma & John Shelor, Richard Shulman, Dhyani Simonini, Maya Tompkins, Elizabeth Tuttle, and Theresa Wright.

And to the numerous people who seek my counsel and ask my advice on meditation, dowsing, energy healing, personal empowerment, spiritual transformation, enlightenment, and so much more. It is to you that I write these words.

Introduction

"I dared not take a breath as I gazed deeply into the mesmerizing eye of the Ancient One. The quiet wisdom that stared back at me was beyond words . . ."

This wasn't some drug-induced hallucinogenic trip. It was a deep meditation that I was enjoying from the comfort of my own living room. I was suddenly and quite unexpectedly whisked away to what felt like an entirely different universe.

I could see and sense that I was in the ocean and the being staring back at me was an Orca. During this "encounter" I received many insights. It was just one of a seemingly endless number of such encounters that I have had over the past 20+ years.

Meditation can literally change your life and set you free!

It allows you to go beyond the confines of the third-dimensional experience with its stress, disharmony, and struggle and enter a world of expanded wisdom, inner peace, and profound insight.

It can help you remember who you truly are which automatically gives life significantly more meaning and purpose.

It assists you in achieving a centered, balanced, and harmonious state of body, mind, and soul.

This state is fertile soil for:

- ❖ physical and emotional healing,
- ❖ harmonious relationships,
- ❖ clear focus and decision making,
- ❖ goal achievement, and
- ❖ a sense of well-being.

Sudden bursts of inspiration come with greater frequency. A sense of inner calm and joy grows ever more prevalent as your meditational practice continues. Your intuition is heightened. Your self-confidence soars. Synchronicity increases. Life begins to flow with significantly more grace and ease.

Peering Through the Veil is about going deep within yourself and finding that calm elation that is considered Nirvana, the promised land, or heaven on earth. It represents breaking through the "Veil of Illusions" you experience being human.

Peering Through the Veil is for those interested in meditation, reducing stress, and feeling more balanced, centered, and peaceful while seeking to awaken more fully into their true spiritual nature and achieve their greatest potential.

It is perfect for both the novice and the experienced meditator. It discusses many different forms of meditation, including the "how to's" for several of the most popular techniques. It also details preparation and enhancements to deepen each experience and gain greater benefit more rapidly.

There are as many ways to meditate and pray, as there are people on the planet. In *Peering Through the Veil,* you will be introduced to, and get to experience, many different forms of meditation. It has been my great pleasure to study, practice, and benefit from each of them over many years.

Meditation is not associated with a particular religion. It is practiced by people from every walk of life, in every religion and on every continent. Regardless of your religious beliefs or practices, meditation can greatly add to your connection and understanding of self and the Divine.

When you read the words "the Divine," feel free to substitute whatever word or phrase you prefer for the Creator of all things. Here are a few choices in no particular order: God, Creator, Divine Mind, Great Spirit, Allah, God Consciousness, Divine Presence, Universal Mind, Goddess, All That Is, Mother Father God . . . *the list goes on.* I've chosen to use the word "God" in several places throughout the text as it is a globally accepted term. I personally prefer "the Divine" or "the Divine Presence."

Meditation and prayer are your way of communicating with God. Your intuition (seen, heard, or felt) is God's response.

Meditation and dowsing are extremely effective ways to enhance your intuition and your ability to understand what the Divine Presence is communicating. They are ways for you to set aside your fears, limiting beliefs, daily hustle and bustle long enough to know and understand the Truth.

The veil of illusion referred to in the title, is made up of the beliefs, fears, judgments, and expectations humans hold that keep them stuck in mediocrity, hopelessness, a desperate longing for something more in life, and a sense of separation from God.

You, the real you, the Divine aspect of Self, is untouched by human emotion and trauma. When you connect with that part of Self through meditation, you breach the barriers *(piercing the veil)* that cause you to feel separate, alone, and sometimes misunderstood.

The Reason You Are Here

The point of being here in the classroom called Earth is to grow, evolve, and become your Divine radiant self ... *what I call the Magnificent Self.* Your life is designed to help you re-member who you are and to express that in every moment.

Meditation is a powerful tool that can assist you in reaching your highest potential. It helps you access and radiate the higher, more Divine, aspects of you. It gives you the courage and confidence to do whatever you set out to accomplish.

Many artistic masterpieces were "inspired." As a person pens a book, creates a symphony, draws or paints, gives inspiring speeches, or works tirelessly for those less fortunate, they often do so from an illuminated place ... *a place of joy and connection with the Divine.*

Sitting alone on a mountaintop, it is easy to maintain the connection with your Divine Self, remaining joyful and at peace, at all times. When you work for a corporation, live in the city, or have to interact with many people every day, staying balanced and peaceful becomes significantly more challenging.

You could be worried about how to pay the rent or you could choose to notice the beauty of the setting sun. It is infinitely easier to find the beauty in life, to experience gratitude and joy regardless of your circumstance when you meditate on a regular basis.

Your Experience with Meditation Will be Unique

You are a unique individual. You have a unique role to play in this world. You have gifts and talents that I may not have. And I have gifts and talents that you may not have. We are both seeking to become our highest potential in our own unique way.

Our life journeys are different. And, therefore, our experiences with meditation will be different as well.

Your times of solitude and meditation will be your own. Certain meditation techniques that I greatly enjoy, you may not, and vice versa.

I do not share my evolutionary journey with you to impress you. As we all have unique and delicious journeys that we have chosen to experience. I share them because humans learn best through story. And, because through story, as you use a different part of the brain to "understand," I am able to help you access the transformational energies and frequencies made available to you by reading this text. These frequencies are designed to assist you in remembering who you truly are ... *the Divinity that you are, the magnificent unique being that you are.*

Practice meditation on a daily basis, heal whatever physical, mental, emotional, or spiritual issues you may face, and you will begin to view and live life in a completely new way.

Discovering Meditation

"Jesus brooded upon the Divine immanence until at last he could declare, I and my Father are One."~ James Allen

# It Begins

At my birth in 1961, I was given the name Deborah Elaine Shelor. My mom was Baptist, a telephone operator turned stay-at-home mom. My father was Lutheran, a mechanical engineer who later became top management at a manufacturing facility.

I mention their religions first because it is what they put first in their lives. My dad chose the name Deborah from a female judge mentioned in the bible.

I had a photographic memory and was an only child.

I Was Called Into Service

I had a life-altering mystical experience at the tender age of fourteen.

I was participating in a non-denominational religious event with a group of teenagers. Suddenly, out of nowhere, a Dove of Light appeared near the ceiling of the sanctuary. We all watched in awe and utter amazement as the Dove slowly descended down from above.

It was the Presence of God (the Divine Feminine, Shekinah, Holy Spirit). It was like a tsunami of energy that flooded the building and everything in it. We were completely consumed in its wake.

Every thought, every cell, every aspect of who we were, was engulfed in the energy. We experienced the feeling of rapture: joy beyond measure, peace beyond words, love everlasting and boundless.

We were literally born again ... into the Light ... *the way they preach about it.* For whatever reason, we received this immense blessing. We had experienced Divinity first hand.

People the world over pray daily for what we experienced so easily and effortlessly that evening. No one could explain why we received this gift and not someone else.

At first, there was silence as we all tried to take in the profound moment we found ourselves experiencing. I began speaking the Language of Light (a.k.a. speaking in tongues). Someone else was "slain in the spirit" and was out cold for almost 45 minutes.

As we each slowly came back to our senses, there was uncontrollable laughter, joy, dancing, and singing. We had literally seen the Light ... *and lived to tell the tale.*

From that moment forth we saw with new eyes and heard with new ears. We no longer had to struggle with the questions most people ponder their entire lives:

❖ Does God Exist?
❖ Is there an afterlife?
❖ Are miracles possible?
❖ Am I worthy to get into heaven?
❖ Is God the judgmental, angry, war-loving father talked of in the Old Testament?
❖ Are the children of Israel the only chosen ones?
❖ Does God love men over women?

We knew the Truth.

Not from reading some book that we had to believe on blind faith, or words spoken by someone "ordained" to teach others how to believe.

Instead, the answers were etched forever within our own hearts.

A Crisis of Faith

Later, as I opened the sacred text whose teachings I knew so well that I could open to the exact passage I was looking for, I realized that several of the teachings no longer rang true.

It failed to bring me the joy and comfort it once had. Instead, reading it now made me angry. It made me sad. I was completely distraught over who I'd been led to believe God is.

The book taught that God chose one tribe over another and was pleased with all the warring and death.

That was definitely not the God I had personally experienced.

The love of the God I experienced is all-pervasive, with no favorites or judgment whatsoever. It was limitless and boundless.

The book says men should obey God and women should obey their husbands.

Again, that is not the God I now knew.

I, along with the others gathered that night, had received God's blessing directly. We came from every walk of life. Some regularly attended church, while others did not. Our backgrounds, social status, and financial situations varied wildly. A few, but not all, had read the sacred book. Some had been baptized, yet there were those who had not been.

Regardless, we had all been engulfed in the Holy Spirit, experienced what it means to know God, and received several spiritual gifts. Gender, age, and religious affiliation had nothing whatsoever to do with it.

Lost in a Spiritual Wasteland

I was not the only one to leave the church soon after that night with the Dove. For a little while, a few weeks, maybe months, the image of the Dove remained above the altar. But slowly It began to fade until eventually it was gone ... *and the tangible feeling of the Presence of God faded from the church right along with it.*

The emptiness I felt when the Dove and the Presence left was almost unbearable. The building was now an empty shell housing nothing but people.

The teachings and the building were now meaningless. I felt they contained neither God nor joy. In fact, now they represented an excruciatingly painful memory of feeling the Presence of God and then having it disappear from my life. This pain was infinitely worse than the loss of human love through break-ups or death. I now completely understood how the Hebrews felt when their temple was destroyed. The Presence would no longer have a place to dwell. It would be years before I realized that the Presence can be housed and experienced within.

The group of us had been forever changed and called into service. Yet we were unsure of how to move forward or what we were supposed to do.

We did the best we could. Many of us ended up simply trying to forget.

Some turned to drugs, sex, and alcohol in an attempt to numb the pain. We were doing whatever it took to pull the veil of forgetfulness back over our eyes. We were wandering around in spiritual darkness.

I tried to run away for a long time. At first, I attempted to forget by drinking way too much in high school and the first couple of years of college. Thankfully, I wised up to the stupidity and destructiveness of such behavior.

Next, I threw myself into one heartbreaking relationship after another while also focusing on my career as an Industrial Engineer and manager.

I was very successfully climbing the corporate ladder. I traveled often and enjoyed what many would consider to be the finer things in life: cruises to the Caribbean; limo rides to black tie affairs in Manhattan; a little red sports car; weekend jaunts skiing in New England, staying in slope-side condo's with fireplaces and Jacuzzis; dinner parties; travel in my company's Learjet; 5 star restaurants and hotels ... *you get the idea.*

But along with material success came severe stress. It was quickly destroying my health and any hopes I had at happiness.

I was one of four managers developing "The Bayer Factory" ... *a state-of-the-art facility and workforce to manufacture Bayer aspirin.* It would be a self-directed work team with the best equipment available anywhere.

Empowering people to work together, teaching them the communication, problem-solving, and technical skills necessary to one day run their department on their own was a dream job for me. But, as has been true on several occasions in my life, all of that changed in the blink of an eye.

It was early one Friday morning. The team leader called me into his office to share the news that the company was doing a major management lay off. Those of us lucky enough (or not) to survive the cut were being reassigned. The Bayer Factory was being disbanded.

My new position was that of a front-line supervisor in another department. Several of my closest friends, business colleagues, and even a few of those in upper management whom I greatly admired had all been let go. It was a devastating day.

And then it became a nightmare.

I hated front-line supervision. It was a job I had refused time and time again. Many companies like their upper management staff to have front line supervisory experience. They feel it makes you a better manager if you understand the nitty-gritty of what happens on the production floor. I was being groomed for upper management, so the job was repeatedly thrust at me.

I'd worked alongside enough supervisors to know that it was not something I was cut out for or desired. People were constantly pulling at you, asking questions, needing immediate assistance, sometimes complaining, whining, or finger pointing. I likened it to babysitting for adults. Whenever the job was offered, I always turned it down.

Yet, here it was, plopped in my lap. I had no real choice ... *be a front line supervisor or find a new job.* I only had the weekend to decide.

Depending on the dynamics between the people on the floor, front line supervision can be deeply rewarding and a lot of fun or it can be like beating your head against a brick wall. Many days for me, it was the latter.

The company decided to implement a plant-wide computer system to track inventory. Computers were being put onto every production line and the material handlers would be doing all the data entry when they brought pallets of packaging components to the line. Many of the people in these positions had never used a computer. It became my job to teach them and to handle implementation on the production floor.

As the system went live, my name was called over the intercom about once every five minutes. I rushed from one data entry disaster to another all day long. Sometimes three or more people stood in line to ask me questions. Every decision I made impacted production for the day. After a year of front-line supervision and implementing this new computer system, one of my employees pulled me aside and told me I looked like I had aged 10 years in the past year. The stress was more than I could bear.

So, I did the only thing left to do . . . *I hit the wall.* I crashed and burned. Term it any way you wish. The bottom line is, I had a complete stress-induced meltdown ...

Remember Who I Am

The Dark Night of the Soul

You've probably heard of the Dark Night of the Soul. I woke up one morning not feeling well and called in sick.

Before I knew it, I was lying on the floor in the fetal position, crying hysterically having vivid flashbacks of being raped. It had happened when I was eighteen.

I was now thirty-three and had never before shed a tear over the event that happened all those years ago. Fifteen years of denial is a very long time!

The emotions I felt were completely foreign to me. I had successfully kept them at bay for 15 years, hiding them from everyone, including myself. But the stress of the job situation caused my fragile emotional egg to crack and the pent-up emotions spilled out everywhere.

I grew up without witnessing strong emotions. I was raised a good southern woman – you grin and bear it, regardless of what "it" is. No one in my family ever expressed anger or fear. I didn't know it was normal to have those feelings. So whenever they were present within me, I just shut them down. That doesn't mean they go away, however. They get stuck in the body and turn into illness. And I'd certainly had more than my fair share of health-related issues.

This dark night brought the intense emotions I'd stuffed all to the surface. Alarmed, I had no reference for the intensity of the anger and fear I was experiencing. I couldn't slow it down or stop it. For the first time in my life, I felt completely out of control. I found that absolutely terrifying. I realized in that moment that if these feelings were a part of who I am, then I didn't really know myself at all.

The Awakening

As odd as it may seem, hitting rock bottom and experiencing that level of sadness and depression was one of the greatest moments of my entire life.

Even though it involved endless tears, an extended leave of absence from work, and several visits to a psychologist, it was one of those rare gateways of transformational opportunity that we are given as humans.

There was no middle ground. I could sink or I could swim. I could become a bitter, lonely, sad, angry, broken soul for the rest of my life or I could soar to greater heights than I ever dreamed possible. I decided it was time to strap on some wings.

In that moment of deepest sadness and despair, I woke up once again to my spiritual nature and began to remember who I Am. I turned to God and asked for help.

A very interesting phenomenon had occurred. Suppressing the rape memory had also completely suppressed my intuition ... *which I later discovered to be one of my most powerful spiritual gifts.*

Following that newly activated intuition, I went for the first time to a New Age bookstore. I picked up a brochure for someone that did Energetic Clearing. I had no idea what that meant, but it felt like the right thing to do and I made the appointment.

It's funny that when the ego is completely shattered, new doorways suddenly appear. Even though I'd abandoned my religion years before, "beware the soothsayers" had haunted me into never stepping foot in one of those shops before.

If I weren't in such a desperate place, I never would have been open to new concepts or alternative therapies and I wouldn't have been so quick to follow my intuition.

But now, here I was.

While I was in the bookstore, I bought an audiotape called *Ocean Dreams* by Dean Evenson. It contained beautiful music and real dolphin sounds. I played it all day, over and over again. The soothing music bathed me with its melodies and the dolphin sounds whispered to my soul. It soothed my pain as I shed fifteen years worth of tears.

When I went for my energy healing session that evening, I was amazed by what transpired. The woman had a stereo and about fifty audiotapes to choose from. The one she played was *Ocean Dreams*. During the session, all I could think about was why this woman chose that audio.

As soon as it was over, I asked her why she chose THAT ONE. She said it was the one she felt I needed.

I was rendered speechless.

That's when I came to the realization that something much bigger was at work and there might actually be something to all this New Age stuff.

I quickly became a regular customer at all the New Age bookstores. I began reading, listening to audiotapes, and attending seminars. I learned about many new things like chakras, the luminous body, metaphysics, flower essences, Taoism, crystals, shamanic journeys, essential oils, Ayurveda, and much more.

Everyone needs a helping guiding hand when their life falls completely apart and they are just beginning their spiritual journey or quest.

The teacher/healer/friend chosen for me was Karen Schweitzer of the *Body Mind Center* in Reading, PA. She saw me through my darkest hours. Through her wise counsel, I was introduced to an endless number of healing modalities and practices. It began with meditation.

At her suggestion, I learned a transcendental form of meditation called *Body Mind Meditation* and began to practice it every day.

Once I "woke up" and finally remembered what I was here for, I dedicated my life to my own personal spiritual unfolding and to helping others. I threw myself wholeheartedly into an accelerated path of spiritual growth and healing. Teachers and experiences magically and synchronistically showed up exactly when they were needed.

My other primary teacher at the time was Stuart Wilde. I had been intuitively guided to read his book called *Affirmations*. I loved it so much that I then read all of his other books and listened repeatedly to his various audio programs.

I did many guided theta meditations with his voice as my guide. I also enjoyed his fabulous 8-day *Warriors in the Mist* program near Taos, New Mexico.

Anyone who begins with Stuart Wilde's teachings is definitely in for an interesting spiritual ride. His methods are rather in your face and always over the top in intensity. I went far and fast in my understanding of spirituality and metaphysics.

Meditating to Stuart's theta metronome audios and doing the *Body Mind Meditation* every day, I developed the ability to drop into a theta brainwave pattern at will. I discuss the benefits of that later on.

Enter the Dolphins

I was learning a great deal about myself and about emotional healing. I felt very drawn to Native American spirituality and turned my second bedroom into a meditation room. In it, I built a huge medicine wheel based on one of the exercises in *Dancing with the Wheel* by Sun Bear and Wabun Wind. It had taken me two months of visiting lapidary shows, crystal and new age shops to purchase all the crystals used in this particular wheel. (You have to remember this was before Google, Amazon, and the ease of buying online). It then took two solid hours to do the ritual dedicating the wheel.

Sitting inside the newly built wheel, I tried a guided visualization meditation for the first time. I discovered that I had an instant affinity for voyaging into alternate realities and could easily experience whatever I was guided to visualize with most of my senses.

The meditation I was following guided me around the medicine wheel in my mind. In each of the four directions, I was to stop and ask for guidance from the energy or animal of that direction. I was amazed at how vivid and real the experience was.

As I worked with the South direction, I very clearly experienced a coyote coming towards me. It then began running around in circles, as if it was chasing its tail. Coyotes are tricksters, and it was pretty funny.

It began to transform and eventually what I saw was a dolphin swimming around in circles. I felt such a rush of joy that I burst into tears. I was feeling completely enveloped and bathed in an exquisite divine healing energy. It felt like a blanket made entirely of unconditional love. I felt wave upon wave of this powerful nurturing energy washing away my sorrows and emotional pain. All I could do in response was weep tears of gratitude and joy.

The moment was truly profound. That was my first dolphin encounter. It spontaneously happened all on its own. After that, dolphins began showing up in all of my guided meditations and I could always feel the healing energy that came with them.

These experiences evolved over time. Initially, I was watching dolphins. Soon I was up close and could sense putting my hand on them. Not long after that, I could feel myself belly to belly with a spinner dolphin. It would torpedo us through the water, spinning all the while.

This spinning through water experience was vastly transformational. I shed tears of joy each time it happened. It felt like years of emotional pain were being released. Afterward, I felt completely cleansed and renewed.

Eventually, I could shapeshift (in my mind) into a dolphin and see through their eyes, or they through mine, whatever the case may be. I was no longer observing them. It was me swimming and leaping through the air with total freedom.

I discovered I could transmit the dolphin healing energy through my body and hands, making it available for others to utilize in order to heal their own emotional wounds.

When the world as I knew it fell completely apart, I reached out to God. I asked for help. I received it ... and *so much more*. God didn't send me his messengers in the form of angels.

No.

I was sent the messengers of the Divine Feminine (the Holy Spirit, Shekinah) in the form of dolphins ... *the angels of the sea*. I was engulfed once again in the all-pervasive energy of love I had felt as a teen when I had my first mystical/spiritual experience. Once again I was able to speak the Language of Light ... *a spiritual gift that began with that first mystical experience with the Dove of Light when I was young.*

As my intuition became more heightened, I began to follow wherever it led. I would read the title of a book and for no apparent logical reason, tears would well up in my eyes. That was my signal to pay attention and buy the book.

The same thing happened when I heard or saw the name of a particular workshop or event. Multiple people would mention a certain teacher, book, or technique, so I would investigate those things further. You'll read about several of those adventures later on.

I was inspired to read hundreds of books, attend numerous workshops, and learn many forms of meditation and healing. I have the equivalent of a Ph.D. in metaphysics from all that training and experience.

I've had many more moments like the Dove in the sanctuary.

Practically every time I attended a workshop, I "received" advanced information about the topic on my way home or right after my morning meditation the following day.

As I was guided to travel and live in different locations, synchronistically meeting people, attending workshops, visiting sacred sites, asking questions, channeling energy and information, spontaneously remembering past lives, doing my own spiritual journey, I was upgraded in vibration, bathed in the Divine healing energy of the Holy Spirit, again and again and again.

Each of these profound moments bringing me to a higher level of wisdom, and making available through me stronger, more powerful, and more highly-refined frequencies for healing,

How I've Changed because of Meditation

Through meditation, dowsing, intuitive guidance and spiritual upliftment with the healing energies that surround and come through me, I've been able to heal much of my emotional wounding from the past. I let go of the emotional pain, sadness, victimhood, and paralyzing fear of rejection that had been so pervasive within me previously.

So much has shifted for me since that fateful day when my world fell completely apart. I've become much more joyful and at peace.

I discovered that the things of greatest value are:

- ❖ love,
- ❖ friendship,
- ❖ happiness,
- ❖ self-worth,
- ❖ inner peace,
- ❖ truth,
- ❖ service, and
- ❖ connection with the Divine.

My psychic, intuitive, and healing abilities have been greatly enhanced. My consciousness and awareness continue to expand. I feel overwhelming joy, love, peace and compassion much of the time.

Eventually, I left the safety and security of the corporate world to head out on my own doing what I love and to make a positive difference in the world.

I receive answers to the questions I ask directly, not from some book or another person, but from within, through my own direct connection to the Divine. It's a connection which you also have, but perhaps have forgotten or were never taught how to fully utilize.

I no longer feel unworthy, hopeless, helpless, fearful, or incomplete. I feel whole. The gaping wound I experienced when the Presence of God could no longer be felt has now been filled. I feel the energy of the Divine Presence often. It surrounds, envelopes, and guides me whenever I seek support.

If you aren't already aware, the Divine Presence is always there for you as well. This book and the accompanying guided meditations are there to assist you in enhancing your connection and awareness of it.

Meditation, for me, has become as natural as breathing. I can click into a different brainwave pattern with or without my eyes closed thanks to years of practice with a method taught by my metaphysical mentor, Stuart Wilde. Sensing and knowing what the

Universe wants me to do or say is something I have spent years perfecting. Countless hours of meditation have played a vital role in fine-tuning that subtle skill.

My spiritual connection has become so strong that I receive help and clear direction about practically everything in life.

You can as well. It just takes dedication to daily spiritual practices like meditation.

Over the past 25 years, I have been repeatedly jolted awake in the middle of the night with Divine insights and inspirations. I receive, through Divine Revelation, healing technologies, meditations, tools, insights, and wisdom.

Based on the new wisdom I've receive, I teach workshops, create extremely high-vibration energy healing tools including Dancing Dolphin Alchemical Synergy products, offer private long distance energy healing/consulting sessions, write books, and share my insights and products throughout the world.

I learned to view life differently. I now see every situation and person as a teacher and an opportunity to learn more about who I am and to become more of what I desire. Even an experience as potentially devastating as divorce allowed me to grow and evolve as a person. I gained poise and confidence instead of being crippled and emotionally destroyed.

The longer I've been consciously on this spiritual journey, the faster and more profound the insights and synchronicities seem to come. I continue to receive new insights and technologies which I feel blessed to share with my readers and clients from all over the globe.

I share these things so you will know that "If I can do it, so can you!"

Benefits of
Meditation

The number and depth of benefits derived from meditation is endless. The most obvious is the letting go of stress. Different forms of meditation affect you differently.

Stress held in the body for too long can lead to dis-ease. Meditation is an extremely effective method of reducing stress. Medical evidence shows that regular practice of meditation lowers blood pressure and improves several other body systems to enhance overall health.

Dr. Herbert Bensen discovered that slowing brain waves down through meditation causes what he calls the "relaxation response." It affects your heart rate, metabolism, blood pressure, respiration, and brain chemistry.

Research studies at UCLA showed that specific areas of the brain were larger in meditators than in non-meditators. A follow-up study at the UCLA Laboratory of Neuro-Imaging found that meditators have stronger neuronal connections between brain regions and less age-related brain shrinkage overall than non-meditators the same age.

On the opposite coast, a Harvard University study found that participating in a mindfulness meditation program caused measurable changes in parts of the brain associated with memory, empathy, stress, and sense of self.

The Harvard study wasn't done with long-term meditators. Subjects practiced guided mindfulness meditations for 8 weeks and the brain showed significant changes in that short time span. Just imagine what can happen with long-term practice.

According to an article by the Mayo Clinic, meditation allows you to:

- ❖ See stressful situations from a new perspective
- ❖ Discover ways to manage your stress
- ❖ Improve self-awareness
- ❖ Learn to focus on the present
- ❖ Lower negative emotions

In the same article, the Mayo Clinic also indicates that meditation has been suggested by some researchers as a way to help with the following conditions:

- ❖ "Allergies
- ❖ Anxiety disorders
- ❖ Asthma
- ❖ Binge eating
- ❖ Cancer
- ❖ Depression
- ❖ Fatigue
- ❖ Heart disease
- ❖ High blood pressure
- ❖ Pain
- ❖ Sleep problems
- ❖ Substance abuse"

As you get into more advanced healing meditations, many more physical issues have the potential to dramatically improve.

In a trance state, a child can be born without the mother experiencing pain, a monk can melt all the snow around him while sitting outside in the frozen winter without a coat, and many more unusual things are possible.

If you meditate first, the "work" just pours forth effortlessly. At least it works that way for me.

It's easier to stay focused, to have inspired creativity guiding me with exactly what to do and say and to get more done if I've meditated. As soon as my meditation time is over, ideas and words to put on paper seem to flow effortlessly.

An incredible state of calm can be reached during meditation. People who meditate regularly experience this calmness spilling over into all parts of their day.

Events or circumstances that once evoked an immediate response of anger or upset begin to have less impact. Eventually, it's like being in the eye of a storm. All around you can be chaos, and yet you remain centered, peaceful, and in joy ... *regardless of the circumstance.*

The real purpose of meditation is to attain and maintain this blissful, peaceful state of being all the time ... *not just while meditating.*

The more you meditate, the more you will experience synchronicity and "flashes of inspiration." You will gain clarity about issues that have been causing you trouble. You will be able to solve problems that you couldn't find solutions to previously. You will link up with more and more people of like mind.

When you go deep within, you can access information and insights that have been hidden from your conscious mind.

Creativity is greatly enhanced. Ideas for creative expression often come while in the alpha or theta mental state ... *which is easily reached with meditation.*

Throughout history, many of the world's greatest inventors turned to meditation for inspiration and problem solving. It's no surprise that they were actively accessing higher wisdom.

I consider myself an alchemist. I care little about transforming base metals from one state to another such as lead

25

into gold. However, I am very interested in what is known as spiritual alchemy ~ the transformation of individuals from a state of disease, poverty, and lack, to a state of health, prosperity, and joy. Meditation is a primary key in that transformational alchemical process.

I invite you to make it a fundamental part of your life. It will provide a firm foundation on which all other parts of your physical, mental, emotional, and spiritual world can be built.

Developing Your Sixth Sense

When I talk about developing your sixth sense, I'm not talking about weird psychic games like séances or Ouija boards ... *which invite "heaven only knows what" into your space.* I'm also not talking about calling a psychic hotline, having your palm read, or listening to a trance channel that is supposedly the voice of some ascended master, alien, dead holy person, or something else.

Much of what's out there along those lines is not only useless, but in some cases actually detrimental.

A few truly clear oracles or channels are out there, but it's very difficult to sift the chaff from the wheat until you have significantly raised your consciousness and developed your own inner knowing. Then it becomes blatantly obvious and you listen to those with wisdom and you run to the nearest exit concerning the rest.

It seems as if people have been consulting oracles, psychics, channels and the like almost since time began. The words of prophets are mentioned in various ancient texts.

The women (Pythia) who acted as Oracles at Delphi were consulted for 1200 years. The great men who heard their prophecies included Socrates, King Croesus of Lydia, Solon, and many more. The Oracle told Phillip II of Macedon that whosoever could ride his spirited colt would be ruler of the world. After many men tried, the only one who could ride it was his own son, Alexander, later called Alexander the Great who did, in fact, conquer most of their known world.

Rulers and Kings have often been depicted with wise men surrounding them.

Several well-known people had readings with the "Sleeping Prophet" named Edgar Cayce. And the result of those meetings made huge differences in their businesses and their lives. Just a few of Cayce's notable clientele:

- Thomas Edison,
- Nikola Tesla,
- Engineers at RCA, IBM, Delco,
- President of the Goodyear Tire and Rubber Company,
- Inventor Mitchell Hastings,
- NBC founder David Sarnoff,
- Irving Berlin,
- George Gershwin,
- Gloria Swanson,
- Ernest Hemingway's mother who consulted him about her son's writing career,
- Marilyn Monroe concerning beauty secrets,
- Nelson Rockefeller,
- And many more.

I am not suggesting you go to someone else for a psychic reading or advice, unless you receive explicit instruction from your internal guidance to do so.

What I'm talking about is you developing your own ability to communicate with Higher Wisdom. Enhance your ability to hear, see, or feel what is happening in the unseen world. Learn to read the signs the Universe is giving you. Follow your inner knowing about things to do or things to avoid.

Strengthen your ability to understand your gut feelings and hunches about companies, investments, places to go, people to trust, etc. When you learn to follow those hunches, great things happen. When you don't, it's pretty much a disaster.

A great example of this is the time I was prompted from within to "go now" to a particular store in Southern California. The moment I walked in the door, I met my future husband, Raven.

Here's another example related to business. Jonathan Goldman and I had been working on a collaboration for several years to infuse his music into my energy healing oil products. He was in Santa Fe for a conference and I had not been able to reach he or his wife, Andi, by phone. I lived just north of Santa Fe and knew that them being in town was the best opportunity for us to nail down the final details of our business agreement.

I was frustrated at not being able to reach them. So, I just said to the Universe, "Jonathan and I need to talk. If it doesn't happen this weekend, it may not ever happen." Once again I heard, "go now."

I grabbed my son, Jess, and headed for town.

As soon as we arrived at the La Fonda Hotel, I went to the conference registration desk to see if anyone knew where Raven was. He was at the conference and I wanted to find out if he had seen Jonathan. While the registration people were discussing the potential whereabouts of my husband, I turned my head to look towards the conference bookstore and saw Jonathan standing in the doorway.

I rushed over and we gave each other a warm embrace. I then told him I wanted to finalize our plans for the chakra kit and other products in the *Essence of Sound* line. We quickly came to an agreement about the details of our arrangement. It took a total of 5 minutes.

Another even more dramatic example of following intuition was my experience of filing for divorce. I absolutely knew that I was supposed to file the papers on a certain day. I can't explain how I knew. I just did. I had insisted that Raven and I have all the paperwork completed in time.

The New Mexican had recently run a long article about do-it-yourself divorce in New Mexico and indicated that it took about two months. More precisely, they said the process takes 51 days.

The day I knew it was supposed to happen, I got up early and made sure the papers were all in order. Raven met me at the bank and my personal banker notarized all the signatures for us. I then took Jess with me to the courthouse. The guy at the window seemed to take forever to organize the papers in the correct order and staple everything together. He then typed a few things into a computer and out popped a name.

He told me that the judge my case had been assigned to was not in that day. So he scribbled something on a teeny tiny little post-it note and handed it to me. He said to go upstairs to either of the judges whose names were on the note and see if one of them could help me.

I thought he must be joking, but apparently, he was not.

I asked Jess to wait for me as I went into the ladies bathroom on the second floor. I entered one of the stalls and dowsed about which judge to ask. Once I had my answer, Jess and I went searching for that judge's office.

The clerk (or whatever her proper title) was very friendly. She took my papers, attached little sticky notes on all the pages that required a signature. Then she handed the papers back to me and said that her judge was out for about an hour and that I should try the other judge. If that judge couldn't help me, then I was to come back a little later.

Now what?

I had been guided to go to the first judge, which I had done. Should I wait for that judge to return or follow the new lead? I knew that sometimes you are given a string of breadcrumbs to follow. As long as you are in complete trust and just follow the trail, it usually comes out O.K. in the end.

I decided to go with what the clerk had suggested. We visited the office of the other judge. His clerk took the paperwork and began to look it over.

I had been at the courthouse for almost an hour and the time was almost up on the parking meter where I had parked outside. I asked the secretary if my son could stay there with her while I fed more quarters into the meter. She said it would be fine.

When I returned to the office, the secretary handed me the paperwork and told me to take it back downstairs to the cashier.

I said, "And then what?"

She replied, "And then you are divorced."

"What?"

I was completely caught off guard. The newspaper had said it took 51 days. I thought I was just dropping off some paperwork and would have to come back in about 2 months to finalize things. But, apparently, while I was putting money in the meter, the judge had signed my divorce papers.

"Seriously?"

"Seriously!"

Woohoo! I was so happy I could hardly contain myself. I called Raven as I skipped down the courthouse stairs and told him, "Congratulations, you are a single man!"

He couldn't believe it.

Neither could anyone else. In fact, no-one has heard of a divorce happening in New Mexico that fast! Most people still don't think it's possible. I've already proven that it is.

I followed my intuition. I absolutely positively KNEW I had to file the paperwork that day. And I did. The results were phenomenal. I was at the courthouse exactly one hour and fifteen minutes.

That's the power of fine-tuning your intuition. You are often in the right place at the right time. And that's when all the magic happens.

Some of the greatest names in recent history have had a strong sixth sense. George Washington and Abraham Lincoln both had visions about the nation and the events that were later to unfold.

Many successful athletes and business people visualize the outcome (which is a form of alpha meditation) before they compete or enter the boardroom.

Now it's your turn . . .

Meditation Preparation

"Meditation brings wisdom; lack of meditation leaves ignorance. Know well what leads you forward and what hold you back, and choose the path that leads to wisdom." ~ Buddha

Meditation
Preparation

Meditation is the time you set aside to reflect, to get to know who you truly are and to commune with Higher Wisdom. It is a form of prayer. And, therefore, the time and location should be treated as sacred.

The following suggestions are designed to help you quiet the mind and slow down the brainwaves so you can go to deeper levels of meditation and Self.

Choose a time and location where you will not be disturbed.

Lighting for Meditation

Any type of soft lighting or candle light instantly assists in calming you down. Turn down the lights, burn only candles, or sit near the fireplace with just the glow from the flames.

I love meditating at the beach at sunrise or sunset. I particularly enjoy meditating at sunrise on the water. I had the wonderful experience of living on board a yacht in the South Pacific. I would get up before anyone else was awake and meditate as the sun was rising.

The only candles I recommend are unscented beeswax. Regular candles are made from paraffin which is a material produced during the refinement of crude oil. Having that in the air, absorbing it through your skin and lungs, is not a healthy choice. The same holds true of the chemical-laden aromas found in most candles.

People often ask me about soy candles and food. Personally, I avoid it. Much soy is genetically modified. Soy was added to monk's diets to tone down their libido. Soy definitely has an effect on your hormones. It may not be the effect you are hoping for.

Music, incense, and calming essential oils add to the depth of any meditational experience. Pure sandalwood is one of my favorites.

Beneficial Scents for Meditation

We each have different preferences on scent.

Personally, I enjoy Triloka brand's Special Sandalwood or Amethyst Balance by Shoyeido (which also contains Sandalwood). Truth is, these are the only two brands and scents I will use. And even those, I only use on rare occasion. I greatly prefer the Dancing Dolphin Products that contain high-quality essential oils.

Many brands of incense and essential oils have toxic chemicals, can give you a headache, and lower your frequency (very undesirable). Toxic chemicals in the air or on your skin can mess up your energy, your health, your vibration, even your ability to absorb nutrients from the foods you eat.

Quality incense, essential oils, and energy elixirs can shift you into a calm, almost euphoric, state and raise your vibration. As with all things, a little goes a very long way. I only burn about 1/3 of a stick of incense at a time. I only diffuse essential oils for about 15 minutes. I never do both at the same time and I typically only do one or the other about once a week.

Music for Meditation

You can play soft, gentle music in the background if you desire. I often use music when leading people through guided meditations. For mantra meditations, music is typically not used.

I don't recommend using music that includes singing or contains words. Your mind will get side-tracked trying to listen. Chanting is an exception. The repetition of sounds can actually assist your mind in slowing down and going deeper.

Musical selections can vary from New Age instrumentals to a shamanic drumbeat to a theta metronome sound. I have included several in the *Resources* section at the back of the book.

Crystal and Tibetan bowls are often used to aid your entrance into a meditative state. Just make sure you enjoy the particular sound, or tone, they make.

I often play a CD that is just a recording of the sea – waves on the shore with the occasional call of a sea gull. Being near the ocean, hearing the sounds live, is even better. I also love to sit near a stream listening to the sound of the water falling over the rocks.

The Perfect Time to Meditate

Whatever time you have is good. Doing it consistently at the same time each day can accelerate the benefits.

Many people choose to meditate at 4 a.m. I did that for two and a half years. It was marvelous. I had to be at work by 6:30 a.m. anyway and I'm a morning person. So the extra bit of time earlier than normal was not that difficult for me.

Yogis often insist that 4 a.m. is best. From a biorhythm perspective, it is the optimal time. Many also say that because most people are still asleep, there is significantly less chaos or "noise" in the air.

It's easier to get a distortion-free connection to God-Mind without all the distractions. That's another reason why out in nature is such a great choice. I love being on the beach at about 5:30 a.m. It's typically just you alone on the beach with the surfers in the water and a few seagulls overhead.

A Word of Caution ~ Do not go alone to places in nature that could be unsafe. Use common sense when choosing a location for your meditations. Sitting, with your eyes closed, going off into a blissful mental state, is not conducive to being fully aware of your surroundings and ready for action should the need arise.

Physical Positioning for Meditation

Remove your shoes:

Part of the purpose of meditation is the movement of energy throughout your body and between you and the world around you. Removing your shoes and wearing loose clothing allows the energy to flow more easily.

Meditation While Lying Down:

Some people like to lie down in a comfortable position on a bed, couch, or on the floor. If it works for you, then great. Many people have the problem of getting so relaxed that they actually fall asleep. Sleeping and meditating are two completely different things. If you need the rest, then go ahead and nap. But to meditate, some people just can't lie down.

I sometimes meditate in bed right after waking up in the morning. I lie on my back with my arms and legs outstretched. I use the hand postures (mudras) described later. Silently I repeat the mantra I was given by my Body Mind Meditation teacher. I then follow that up with a mantra I received myself. You will read more about mudras and mantras later on.

Meditating on the Floor:

Sit directly on the floor or on a cushion with your legs crossed, or any other way that is comfortable. The lotus position in yoga is not necessary to achieve a quiet and peaceful state and most people can't do it comfortably anyway.

Meditating on a Chair:

The most comfortable position for most people is to meditate on the couch or on a comfortable chair. Keep your legs uncrossed and feet flat on the floor ... *unless this is uncomfortable.*

Sometimes when I meditate on a couch or chair with no arms, I put my feet up and cross my legs the same way I would if I were seated on the ground or floor.

Meditation Posture:

Keep your back as straight as you comfortably can. Energy travels through the spine ... *so you want to keep that channel clear.* There are wonderful meditation cushions available that can greatly assist.

Placing Your Tongue for Meditation:

Gently place your tongue on the little flat place on the roof of your mouth just behind your front teeth. This closes an energy circuit inside your body. Keep it lightly pressed there during the entire meditation. This will allow you to go much deeper and will assist in calming your mind.

Because of how effective this is to calm the mind, I find that I do it a great deal, even when I am not meditating.

Hand Positions for Meditation:

Using a mudra *(a particular hand position)* enhances how the energy flows through the body. This greatly affects your mental state, which accelerates your ability to achieve a deep level of meditation.

In this image, my son, Jess, is showing the mudra typically done with a mantra meditation. With the left hand, form a circle by touching the tip of your thumb to the tip of your index finger and extend out straight the remaining 3 fingers. Repeat this with the right hand. With your hands comfortably in this position, place your hands on your thighs or down at your sides.

In the next image, I am doing another mudra. The "prayer position" is also a powerful way to activate many of the energy centers in your hands.

This one is tiring to do for 20 minutes if you are seated. I often do this one while lying down resting my hands on my chest.

Different mudras do different things. Play around with your hand positions.

Try a new one each time you meditate and see what a difference it makes in the ease of calming your mind, in the alignment of your spine, in the insights you receive, etc.

Close your eyes:

Once you have started meditating, it is best to stay in the same position if at all possible. Starting out being comfortable, therefore, is very important. It's O.K. to move if you absolutely must. Staying in one comfortable position is much preferred.

Now you know the basics of how to prepare. Let's take it up a notch and talk about sacred space.

Setting Sacred Space

For thousands of years, people all over the globe have created sacred spaces in which to meditate and perform other religious and spiritual practices. These include churches, mosques, and other religious temples; kivas, sweatlodges, and medicine wheels used by indigenous cultures, standing stone circles, even the dance grounds used by whirling dervishes and native dancers.

Does it make a difference?

Absolutely!

This image is of the LOTUS (Light of Truth Shrine) at Yogaville in Virginia. The lower level of the lotus shrine honors all religious teachings from around the world. The upper level is a place for silent prayer and meditation.

Creating Your Own Sacred Space

One of the easiest and most effective ways to create sacred space is using a medicine wheel. I tell you how in a later chapter. It acts as a portal to Higher Wisdom.

Another option is to create a sacred altar or shrine inside your home or out in your garden. An altar is simply a place set aside for items that have spiritual significance to you. The altar is usually set up near the cushion or chair where you meditate regularly.

Your altar can be as elaborate or simple as you desire. There is no right way or wrong way to create one.

A religious person might place a copy of their sacred text or a symbol of their religion on their altar. Often people arrange candles, crystals, fresh flowers, or images on the table, dresser, or other space they have set aside.

My son has a portable Buddhist shrine. It is a box carved out of wood. When opened, it has a carved image of Buddha sitting with wooden panels flanking both sides. It looks like a miniature version of the inside of a Buddhist temple.

Most people who practice spirituality end up creating sacred space throughout their home. In practically every room they play soft uplifting music and they place pictures, crystals, candles, tapestries, fresh flowers, and fountains throughout. The moment you walk through the front door, it feels like you have entered sacred space. It feels like that because you have.

Once you have set up an altar or shrine, close your eyes and say your intention for the space out loud. Ask that it be made sacred and that it be a place of healing, upliftment, and peace. Add in any other desires you have for the space.

You might want to be careful what you ask for though.

Soon after my former husband, Raven, and I moved to our new property in New Mexico, we invited over a group of friends to help build the sweatlodge. I also had them come into what I called The Sanctuary to dedicate that new space as well.

The Sanctuary was a beautiful secluded outdoor garden with raised flower beds, fountains, and wonderful shade trees. We stood in a circle holding hands and each person took their turn making a statement about the sacredness of the place. I said that I wanted the space to uplift everyone who entered and that I wanted it to be as if they had entered an entirely different reality, like Camelot, a magical healing place where there was a noticeable difference from their normal everyday life.

A few hours later, one of our friends took time out to do a meditation, and she ended up having a conversation with a dragon. It seems that the Pendragons, one white and one red, had come to inhabit the space. My words had invited them there.

I know the idea of dragons sounds truly absurd. But she wasn't the only one. On more than one occasion, several people experienced dragons in The Sanctuary and Raven's Earth Sky Sweat Lodge. Many who came to visit never seemed to want to leave. It felt great to be at our place. We even had people show up and pitch tents, staying sometimes for days. We often had people fly in from Europe and many other locations to participate in the lodge and spend time in The Sanctuary.

Energy Vortexes

Sacred spaces often exist naturally. These include areas with energy vortexes as well as some old-growth forests, high mountains, and cliffs.

Ancient people often erected a temple in those locations. Many of them have now been covered over by a church.

People flock to many of the famous vortex locations like Stonehenge in England, Sedona in Arizona, Machu Picchu in Peru; Mt. Shasta in California, Chichen Itza in Mexico; Chimayo in New Mexico, and so many others.

The first home Raven and I rented was on an energy vortex. We lived on top of Palomar Mountain in southern California, near the Palomar Observatory, home of the Hale Telescope.

We found out about the vortex quite by accident. Raven had attended a workshop taught by Drunvalo Melchizedek. Drunvalo had indicated that the earth's pole was shifting so significantly, that if you took a compass, placed it in a particular spot and marked due North, that if you came back a month later, the arrow would have moved to a new North location.

We were very curious to see if that was true. Raven walked around the house holding the compass trying to determine a good place to put it and leave it for a month. As his hand went past my chair at the kitchen table, the compass needle began to spin quickly around and around. It never stopped. Of course, there might have been a more logical or scientific reason for the spinning compass. But we were never able to discover such a reason ... *even though I am an engineer and know how to look for such things.*

An interesting and humorous side note: Palomar Mt. is rumored to have had the highest number of UFO sightings of any location on earth until the mid 80's when they abruptly stopped. We didn't know that until after we had moved there.

Past Life Memories

On more than one occasion, I found myself having spontaneous past life memories while visiting some location with a powerful vortex. This type of information is simply easier to access when there is more spiritual energy present.

I'll never forget the day I was talking to Raven, and suddenly burst into tears saying, "We're moving to Chimayo on Easter Sunday!"

O.K. that was just plain strange. And not at all normal ... *even for me!*

What on earth was I talking about?

At the time, I had no idea. And neither did he.

It was Easter Sunday. We had recently sold our home in Canada, packed everything we owned into a big U-Haul truck with my little red sports car pulled behind, and headed down the road from Toronto to New Mexico.

We knew no-one in New Mexico. We didn't know where we were going to "land." We just knew that it was where we were supposed to be.

I guess I'll have to back up a bit in order for you to understand the significance of the story.

Raven and I were new parents living in Whidby, Ontario, a suburb of Toronto. We met while living in southern California and were missing the sun and warmth.

We took a much-needed vacation from the frozen Canadian winter to San Diego. While we were there, Raven suddenly had an "inspiration" to contact an immigration lawyer. We were living in Toronto because Raven is Canadian and could easily get a job there.

We had already been to the American Consulate in Toronto trying to determine the procedures and paperwork necessary so that we could move to the United States.

It was a pretty unappealing system.

47

You had to complete a bunch of paperwork and pay a lot of money. It would take six months to a year to be approved and then once it was approved, you only had six months to move to the states or you would forfeit the whole thing. Well, who could make plans under circumstances like that? We had not figured out how. So we had not started the paperwork, even though we knew we wanted to live in the States.

While we were on vacation in San Diego, Raven went to see an immigration lawyer. Being a former cop, he knew that there were "the rules" and there was usually some type of loophole or exception that most people know nothing about.

Sure enough, the lawyer said that there was an exception. If you were married to an American citizen and were visiting the states on vacation and decided to stay, they would let you.

He cautioned, though, that if we decided to take the loophole we would have to actually stay now. According to the lawyer, if we went back to Canada to get all our affairs in order and tried to come back and do it later, it wouldn't work.

We both knew immediately that we were moving to the U.S. ~ not in six months to a year, but now. Right now.

Wow!

We were very surprised and excited.

Raven was head of security at the main branch of the largest bank in Canada. He had to call his boss and tell him that he wouldn't be reporting to work on Monday . . . or ever.

We didn't feel good about that call. It was a great job, and he had a wonderful boss. But this was about the rest of our lives. And we knew we didn't want to live it in Toronto.

Once the paperwork was started, Raven couldn't leave the U.S. We were only there on vacation. We didn't even have our own vehicle. We had been driving a rental.

There was a lot to do.

I flew back to Canada with our young son and set about selling our home. Once it was listed, it sold in two weeks for the price we wanted.

It seemed that the Universe was behind us on this decision.

Suddenly things got more than a little squirrely.

Raven was in California looking for a home, a job, and a truck. He thought he had successfully found all three. So, I sent a check for $10,000 as a down payment for the truck and some fee for the house.

The check never arrived.

Yikes!

I don't know if you've ever lost $10,000, but how you handle situations like that can show you a lot about yourself.

When I "tuned in," I simply knew everything would be alright. I trusted that the Universe was guiding us, and whatever was supposed to happen would reveal itself.

I had already been meditating for several years which allowed me to remain calm, at peace, and clear-headed in situations such as that. A "normal" person would have been completely freaked out and probably quite irrational.

When you are worried about something, it is practically impossible to make good decisions. The fear grips you in its iron fist and forces you to tense your muscles, obsess over the thing being worried about, and lose sight of the bigger picture. You become constricted. It is as if you hunch over and look down only seeing the thing you are worried about.

If on the other hand, you could still your mind and emotions, remaining calm and centered, then you would be aware of the infinite number of options available for solving the issue at hand. Meditation allows you to hold that calm centered place within yourself, even under duress.

Back to the story . . .

There was a deadline for making these payments. The date came and went and the check never showed up.

We took it as a sign from the Universe that maybe Southern California wasn't where we were supposed to be.

It was obvious that moving to the states was the right course of action.

The loophole about how had been revealed to us. The house in Canada sold immediately. Raven's U.S. paperwork went through and was approved at lightning speed. He could now legally work in the U.S., and he was no longer stuck in California. He was free to leave anytime he wanted to.

We felt the Universe was definitely behind the move.

But when the money didn't show up and the deadlines were missed, we started thinking that maybe we should be looking somewhere else. And, just as I expected, after the deadlines were over, the missing check magically arrived.

I told Raven that he had to come back to Toronto. Where to move was a decision too significant to figure out by phone. I wanted to look him in the eyes and make the decision together.

Once he got back to Toronto, we laid out a giant map of the United States on a table. He stood on one side and I on the other. We both stared at the map intently for awhile without speaking.

Suddenly we both looked up at exactly the same time and said, "New Mexico." For me, the word New Mexico seemed to glow on the map when I looked at it.

I see the same glow around a flower when I'm to use that bloom when making a flower essence. I had seen that same glow around the word San Diego on a map before I moved there and soon after met Raven.

Enhancing my extrasensory perception through meditation and dowsing allows me to get the messages the Universe is sending. It will help you that way as well.

So that's how we ended up in New Mexico.

We were now downtown Santa Fe looking for a place to live. We called numerous people with listings in the paper offering houses for rent.

No one called us back. It was Easter weekend.

Finally, we got one call at our hotel.

As we were driving out of Santa Fe heading north to see that property, I blurted out about moving to Chimayo on Easter Sunday.

Sure enough, we met the owner, took one look at the place, and said we'd like to rent it. We began moving in. It was Easter Sunday and Chimayo was right up the road.

El Santuario de Chimayo was built on a huge vortex in a spot where a crucifix was found in the sand. The crucifix was taken from the spot in the sand over to the Catholic Church that had been erected at San Juan Pueblo. They placed it in the church there and it somehow disappeared. They found it again at the same spot in the sand. I believe the story goes that they took it back to the church and again it disappeared, once again appearing at the spot in Chimayo. By then they decided that God wanted a church built there and the Santuario was constructed in Chimayo in the early 1800's.

Each year during the holy week before Easter, some 30,000 or so people pilgrimage to the Santuario.

In ages past, it was considered the Lourdes of America and many miraculous healings apparently happened for those who made the pilgrimage. They said the sand had a healing effect. There is an antechamber that used to have crutches and other things hanging on the wall from the miraculous healings of the past.

I lived in the little hamlet of Nambe, about six miles from Chimayo, and I never heard of any miraculous healing happening the nine years that I lived there. I did hear about two teenagers who were shot while on a pilgrimage to Chimayo by a jealous former boyfriend.

Where there is light, sometimes there is also darkness. In addition to being a beacon for Catholic seekers, Chimayo is also known as the heroin capital of the United States. It's a funky little town, like many in New Mexico, that make you look around and wonder if perhaps you've taken a wrong turn and ended up in a third world country some place.

The vortex is very real. The Santuario is actually out on a spiral emanating from the center of the vortex and not at the center of the vortex itself. I have been to the vortex center many times. There is a large stone above the vortex and when I closed my eyes and put my hand on it for the first time, I saw visions of a past life where I lived somewhere on a prairie.

Vortex locations allow you to access lots of things you would not normally be able to access.

I had a similar experience in Sedona, Arizona on one of my visits there. Sedona is famous for its vortexes. So famous in fact, that a company with pink jeeps will drive you around with a private guide and show them to you.

Ah, don't ya just love capitalism?

I was hiking along a trail near Sedona, following a friend. When I looked down, it was as if I could see and feel myself as a native woman wearing moccasins and a buckskin dress. That feeling and imagery stayed with me for about half an hour as I walked through that particular forest and climbed up on some large boulders to meditate with my friend.

He and I sat cross-legged facing one another holding hands atop the giant boulder. We closed our eyes and began to meditate. Periodically we would open our eyes and change hand positions. Each time we did this, when we closed our eyes again, we saw (remembered) a different past life with one another. Moving our hands from one position to another was much like changing the channel on a television. The amplifying vortex energy of Sedona definitely made this possible.

My intuition normally functions as a feeling or an inner knowing. The ability to see in the unseen is not my usual gift. At sacred sites, some powerful vortex locations, and during certain forms of meditation, I can often see or hear things that I would not normally be able to.

As you experience powerful locations and sample different forms of meditation, perhaps you will spontaneously remember past lives as well.

 # Spiritual Pilgrimage

I f you feel inexplicably drawn to visit a particular place, a powerful energy or experience could be waiting for you there. You may have a memory or an insight by following that hunch that you would not have had otherwise.

Every moment of your life is part of your spiritual evolution. Your life is your personal quest for the Holy Grail. Every person and situation you encounter is there to show you something about yourself or something you believe. Often situations show up in your life to show you what you judge.

When you are on "pilgrimage," you are outside your normal life experience. You are away from home and the things and people you experience every day. You have to deal with new people and situations. And you get to stop thinking or worrying about the "normal" experiences you typically face. This allows you to view life from a new perspective and experience things you might not while in the comfort and security of your usual surroundings.

A true pilgrimage, with the potential to change your life, has to include you getting out of your comfort zone and dealing with unexpected situations. Often they are done alone and in silence. Basically, they are like a moving sweatlodge or vision quest. You never know what is going to happen. There is often physical hardship and sometimes even danger. And often, somewhere along your way, there is a battle. Typically the battle is within. Should I do this? Or should I do that? Should I give up?

A knight heads out on a quest. He faces danger and new situations at every turn. He may never find his way back to his village. He must overcome his fears and learn to trust himself and God in order to survive. Who he becomes and the skills he develops along the way are the stuff of legend. That is the Divine alchemy, the transformation of lead into gold, the attainment of the Holy Grail of self.

You are the knight. Your life is your quest.

I mentioned earlier that I used to live only a few miles from Chimayo, NM. People pilgrimage there by the thousands each year. What I observed most of these people doing did not contain the ingredients necessary for what I consider a true pilgrimage.

Many of the people walking miles to Chimayo are often talking the whole time on their cell phones or going in packs and joking with their friends. There is no inner reflection going on. They are not facing the unknown and the elements on their own like a knight on a quest. Instead, every few miles there is a designated stop with first aid, water, and bathrooms. The path is all paved now, clearly marked with signs and caution lights. If you can't finish the journey, you simply call someone on your cell phone to pick you up.

Anything new and out of your comfort zone can be a sacred journey. Getting married, moving to a new town or country, getting a new job, or starting your own business are all potential spiritual adventures.

Pregnancy is one of my favorite Rites of Passage or Initiation situations that is definitely a sacred journey. Unlike many other situations, the woman can't change her mind and bail once she is in labor. It is a situation she must face and must move through to completion. And she must do it alone. Yes, she can have external help. But she must have the baby. No one can do it for her.

It can be tough, arduous, and even life threatening. It can also be ecstatic, glorious, and pain-free. Pregnancy and motherhood are powerful spiritual journeys. They allow a woman to become so much more than she would ever be without that experience.

Pilgrimage-related meditations can be truly profound and life changing. When you go to a spiritual workshop, swim with dolphins, or on vacation to Sedona or another sacred location, you go there expecting miracles.

Mt. Shasta

I was very excited to be heading to Bimini, one of the Bahamas out islands, to co-lead a week of wild dolphin swimming and spiritual training. The trip had quickly filled with participants. It would be my first time with dolphins in the wild. Dolphins had

been coming to me for years in meditation. I had yet to swim with them in water.

One morning while meditating I received the insight that the Wesak (Vesakha) festival that year was very important.

Wesak is commonly referred to as Buddha's birthday. It is actually a celebration of his entire life from birth, through enlightenment, to his transition into the afterlife. It is a powerful energetic window through which the Buddha returns each year to bless humanity.

I knew very little about it at the time.

Raven and I were not card-carrying members of any religion. I made the conscious decision to leave the church years before.

I studied many spiritual traditions and mystical teachings from around the world along with the information I receive directly from the Divine. Raven was drawn to earth-based spirituality and Taoism. When our son very clearly enunciated "Buddha" as his first spoken word, I decided Buddhism was something I should learn more about.

For years I had heard about the Wesak festival held at Mt. Shasta in California. It was a weekend celebration facilitated by Dr. Joshua David Stone. Every time I saw a flier or was reminded through an ad or heard a comment about the event, when I "tuned in," I got no signal indicating it was something I needed to do. I had, therefore, written it off years before.

Now, suddenly, I received through what I call Divine Revelation (inner guidance) that Wesak that year was important. I got out my pendulum and began asking questions. I was trying to determine if it was simply the time period that was important or if it was the festival held in California. I got that it was the actual celebration in California was something I should pay attention to.

I checked out the dates of the festival and they fell the weekend the Bimini trip was ending. There was no way I could be in Bimini and Mt. Shasta at the same time.

Now what?

I had to just let it go. When you know you don't have enough information to figure it out with your logical mind, the best course of action is just to let it go and stop trying to figure it out.

A week or two later I woke up knowing I wasn't going on the trip to Bimini. I was shocked, hugely disappointed, and more than a little apprehensive about calling my trip co-facilitator, Amanda, to tell her the news.

How do you say to someone that you aren't going on a trip that you are co-leading and that you filled with your own newsletter readers? And then how do you explain that you don't have a logical reason why you are not going, just that your internal guidance is that you are not?

I called Amanda. As soon as I started explaining that I wouldn't be going, she piped in saying, "I already know. I got it in meditation this morning."

Whew.

At least I didn't have to try to justify my completely irrational actions.

And isn't it wonderful that others who meditate can also receive information making your relationship with them easier?

Meditation can be such a gift.

O.K. So I'm not going to Bimini. Then it must be time to plan a trip to Mt. Shasta. As I dowsed about this, I got, "No!"

I became a bit frustrated and somewhat confused. O.K. I'm not going to Bimini ~ a trip I REALLY wanted to go on so I could finally swim with dolphins for the first time. And yet I'm not supposed to plan a trip to Mt. Shasta and get tickets for the festival. Ugh.

All I could do was trust.

I made the announcement to the Bimini trip attendees that I would not be joining them. And then I went on with my normal routine.

I had planned an ad for Dancing Dolphin Essences through the StarDoves network. The agreement I had with Raja, my friend and head of the network, was that I would send the ad to him. He would look it over. He would then send it back to me with suggestions about ways to improve it. I would make the changes and then send it along with an article I wanted published with the ad.

So I sent Raja the ad. Within a few minutes, I received it in my inbox. He had sent the ad out through the network.

Oh no!

That wasn't at all what we had talked about. He had forgotten that he had agreed to just look it over. Since we had talked about all of that, it never occurred to me that I needed to mention it again in the email to him.

Now it was too late.

He had already sent it. It would be no good to fix it up and send it out again with an article. It was already out there. I sent off an email to Raja letting him know what had happened.

He wrote back a very sweet apology and asked if I'd like two free tickets to the Wesak Festival as a consolation ... *a $600 value.* Raja was one of the organizers. He did much of the advertising for Dr. Stone.

Wow.

Who knew?

I could not possibly have seen that coming even if I'd had a crystal ball.

It is sometimes difficult to simply follow instructions, especially when they don't make any logical sense to you, and trust that the Universe knows exactly what it's doing. But the more situations that occur like this in your life, the easier it becomes. All you need is the courage to trust your inner wisdom and your connection to the Divine Presence.

What at first seemed like a problem, was actually a divinely orchestrated key event in the unfolding of this spiritual saga. *(For those who have a spirituality related business, the StarDoves network is a fabulous place to advertise.)*

I wasn't supposed to plan and pay for my trip to Mt. Shasta because it was being handed to me on a silver platter. Free tickets to the festival were now mine.

Soon I had another problem, though. Raven and I were seriously considering moving to Northern California or Southern Oregon. We had decided that I should take time during this trip to Shasta to scout out potential new locations to live. I would need several extra days and Raven couldn't be off work that long.

I needed a travel companion.

I called all of my dearest friends. Not one person in my inner circle was available for the journey. I felt like I was running out of options.

Raven just sort of sternly said to me, "Who is your best friend that you want to do this trip with?"

Out of my mouth came the name, "Samone."

Well, that was unexpected.

She certainly wasn't one of my best friends. In fact, we hardly knew each other. We traveled similar circles in Santa Fe, but we had never spent much time together.

I believe in synchronicity and following signs so I called her up and asked her what she was doing during the dates of the festival.

She started laughing saying that she was supposed to be on a trip to Arizona, but had run into a glitch. Her Corvette needed major repairs that cost more than expected. She had canceled her trip to Arizona.

So . . . she was available and thought it sounded like a very fun adventure.

Samone's business partner, Susan, made crystal items to sell. I had the entire Dancing Dolphin Essence line plus a few other products that I offer through my websites. Anyone who had tickets to the festival could set up a booth and sell their wares. We piled ourselves and all our items for sale into my Jeep Cherokee and headed off into the sunset. Between the essences and the crystals, the Jeep was literally buzzing from all the energy.

It turned out to be quite the journey. So many things happened on so many levels that it could easily fill a book. Maybe one day I will write about the whole adventure.

But for now, I'll share with you two of the events that happened in Shasta and why I absolutely had to be there during the celebration.

Samone and I were at the festival grounds with our booth on the lawn outside. I was 100 feet from the entrance to the lecture hall and never once set foot in the place. I simply never felt guided to do so.

I'm sure that the lectures, meditations, and music were uplifting, food for thought, and entertaining. But I only read and participate in things my inner wisdom guides me to.

The wrong information can totally screw up your understanding and take you off course. It is sometimes difficult to read a book, attend a lecture, or participate in a meditation with others, and not take all of it as gospel truth. Most things are only 50% true. Many things are even less.

If you read it, hear it, or have your energy field and subconscious mind exposed to it, it can be quite difficult to recognize and release the false bits. It is hard for most people to determine what is and what is not true. I'm actually fairly good at that because of my pronounced inner knowing. But it does take time and effort to be "tuned in" all the time. So, I simply don't expose myself to things of a spiritual nature unless I'm guided to do so.

I'm not talking about things I do for entertainment. I'm talking about the things I read or attend that are connected to my areas of expertise - spirituality, energy healing, and achieving personal magnificence.

Back to the story . . .

No one bothered to tell us that Mt. Shasta is notorious for high winds. Seventy-mile-per-hour wind there is apparently not uncommon. The weekend of the festival, it drizzled rain on and off most of the time, and the wind was wicked.

It was so cold and damp Saturday afternoon that we decided to abandon the booth. Few people were venturing outside the warmth and comfort of the lecture hall to visit the booths anyway. We packed up the most valuable items, stuck them in the jeep, and headed to the mountain.

Mt. Shasta is a beautifully snow-capped sacred mountain. Like Sedona, Stonehenge, and the pyramids at Giza, it is a location where many spiritually-minded people travel seeking Higher

Wisdom. We drove all over it looking for a place to hike and do a meditation. Nothing seemed quite right.

I kept feeling drawn to the mountain peak next to it. It is somewhat pyramid-shaped and very dark in color. I have no idea what type of stones are on it or the particulars of the mountain, but it definitely drew me in. We found a hiking trail nearby and headed off.

A couple of locations seemed suitable for our meditation. Yet none of them were "it." I started thinking, "If I have been here before, where would I go?" I immediately realized I would go "up." So we found a small rise in the terrain and climbed the hill. At the top of the rise was an indentation about two feet deep and six or so feet in diameter. It was perfect. In fact, it felt like the "doorway" to the mountain.

We set up an elaborate grid of crystals and sacred geometry. I don't typically do all of that, but it was definitely what we were being guided to do for this particular meditation.

We sat down cross-legged facing one another, closed our eyes, and entered the silence. So much energy began pouring into me that my body began to vibrate, my back kept arching and my body felt like it was being pushed backward.

Samone is clairvoyant (the ability to see energy) and looked with her inner eye to see what was happening. She saw Mother Mary standing behind me with her cloak opened and encircling me on all sides. The energy I was being enveloped in was coming from her robe.

This energetic upgrade, download, or initiation, depending on how you prefer to language it, went on for quite some time. It was the first of two powerful energetic experiences I was to have at Mt. Shasta.

I shared before how I never went into the lecture hall at the Wesak festival. Samone didn't either, with one exception.

The next day, in addition to the weather being cold, windy and generally inhospitable, it was also raining. We put up the side canvases on the display tent to block the wind and rain. It was actually quite cozy inside.

Samone decided to check out James Twyman's performance and see what was happening inside at the festival. Just as she was ducking out, someone else was ducking into our display tent to get out of the rain.

The man looked around at the various things we had to sell. Every time I asked him a question, he moved his body in this weird fashion. For a little while, I wondered if he was having seizures of some kind.

Between odd movements we began to talk.

It turns out that the guy, Don McInnes, was from New Zealand. He had been told that there was a mission for him in America. Of course, he had free will and could choose not to go, but he was needed during the Wesak celebration in California.

He and a few friends made reservations and headed to the U.S. Now here he was standing in my tent, moving his body this way and that as a way of stepping down the energy so that I could handle it when it came my way. If the energy had simply been directed at me without this step-down process, then it could have fried my circuits ~ burning through my nervous system and I wouldn't have been able to utilize and benefit from it. He acts like a human transducer, altering the energy so it's usable by others. He calls himself a body electrician.

I won't get into how all that works in this book, but I have had several experiences like this, and it can be very physically damaging for those who are unprepared. I don't know if you know any trance channels, but many of them quickly age and their health often fails very rapidly. It's because the frequencies they are bringing in are so much higher and more powerful than their body and nervous system, in particular, is prepared to handle.

I have actually taught many channels how to refine their body through nutrition, certain meditations and several tools I've been given to assist. But this event happened long before I started working with channels and before I had some of the knowledge necessary to create the tools to help them.

Don told me I had to drink lots of water in order to receive the energy. So I poured a glass. As soon as the glass was empty, his body movements would stop and he would say, "Keep drinking." I literally drank over a gallon of water while he continued to step down energy for me. This went on for a good hour and a half to two hours.

Somewhere in the middle, Samone came back into the booth. She immediately went into spiritual warrior mode, clicking quickly into her psychic vision to see what the heck this guy was doing. She followed the energy going from him to me and then from him up. She saw Beings of Light literally pouring blue light energy out of what looked like a pitcher down onto Don and then it went to me in a smaller stream.

As soon as she had tuned into it, she began receiving it as well.

We were literally being bathed in Divine healing blue light.

Our meditation the day before had been a beautiful preparation for the receiving of this gift. These two energy experiences were the reason I needed to be in Mt. Shasta during the Wesak festival and why Don had flown all the way from New Zealand.

Had either of us not listened to our inner knowing, the moment would not have happened.

He and I are now very dear friends.

Later that summer I did get to co-lead a trip to Bimini to swim with wild dolphins. That, too, was a powerful sacred journey in which I received many gifts and insights. I'll share a bit about it in the next chapter.

Meditation & The Brain

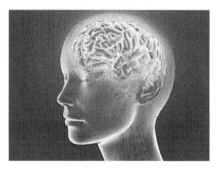

As you meditate, your brain changes state. It calms down. It becomes quiet. Stray thoughts fall away. You find peace, clarity, and pinpointed focus.

There are six commonly described brain activity states: beta, alpha, theta, delta, gamma, and mu. There are probably others. We just have no way of measuring them yet.

Brainwaves look like a sound wave undulating up and down on an EEG (electro-encephalograph) chart. They are measured in Hertz (Hz) or cycles per second. The numbers associated with various brainwave states vary somewhat depending on the researcher.

Beta is you, wide awake, having a conversation, or just going about your day. When you never relax, but stay in beta all the time, you can have trouble remembering things, experience higher blood pressure and respiration, have a hard time concentrating, and difficulty being creative. Anxiety and stress happen here as well. Beta brainwaves fall in the 12 to 30 Hz range.

Alpha is a more relaxed state where the brain speed slows down. Stress relief, relaxation, and regeneration begin here. So does creativity and concentrated focus. Young children spend most of their time with their brain in alpha. Alpha happens in the 8 to 12 Hz range.

Theta is a deeper state. The brain activity is slowed down even more. It is associated with drowsiness. According to Stuart Wilde, visualization in Theta is typically black and white. That's one of the ways you know your brain is operating in theta. Theta occurs in the 4 to 7 Hz range.

Delta is usually totally asleep. Babies tend to have a lot of delta brain wave activity. Few adults are able to remain conscious if their brain speeds have slowed to delta.

Although I haven't achieved it yet myself, I've heard that the ability to teleport – literally dematerialize your body in one location and materialize it in another (instant transportation) – happens in Delta.

Since I've never seen anyone actually dematerialize, much less seen anyone dematerialize while hooked up to an EEG machine, I'll leave that for you to decide.

Delta brainwaves range from zero to 4 Hz.

Gamma is a heightened awareness state. Gamma brainwaves occur in the 30 to 100+ Hz range.

Mu is another brainwave pattern that is associated with the sensorimotor cortex. It happens in the 8 to 13 Hz range. There is speculation that autism has something to do with this brain wave pattern. Much research is still to be done in this area.

Deep meditation for just 20 minutes, allowing your brain state to slow down to alpha, theta, or even delta, can have the same effect on the body as several hours of sleep. Energy is restored. Repair and healing can take place. Stress is reduced and a whole host of other healthy benefits occur.

Most people are in one brain wave state or another. They go from fully awake, to relaxed and creative, to slower and more ready to sink into sleep.

By using EEG machines, researchers have discovered that people drop from Beta to Alpha, then Theta, and finally Delta as they are falling asleep. While sleeping, your brainwave patterns change as you go through stages of dreaming and not dreaming.

Sometimes when a person is meditating, they drop very deep very fast. It's as if they have gone from Beta right to Delta with nothing in between. I've only seen this happen with people who have been meditating for years and do a lot of shamanic work.

The first time I saw it happen was when my friend, Loma, was communicating with dragons at my house. I mentioned it briefly in an earlier chapter. She had gone inside and fell asleep in the middle of my living room floor.

That in itself made me laugh. We had couches and numerous beds to choose from. I thought it was kind of odd that she chose the middle of the main room and walkway. She had been in there for almost an hour, and I decided it was time to check on her.

When I tried to wake her up, she wouldn't move. She was so deep that her consciousness was just not in her body. She was somewhere else. It was as if she was in a coma. I just sat there on the floor with her until suddenly she sat bolt upright, looked right through me as if I wasn't there, and said in a very odd voice, "There are dragons here."

It was all I could do to not burst out laughing. The whole thing was so dramatic, I found it completely hysterical. I did the best I could to talk without laughing, and I said, "Are they nice dragons?"

She looked at me with a very serious expression on her face and said, "Nice isn't a word I would use to describe dragons."

"Em, O.K."

Ah, it was funny.

Wild Dolphins in Bimini

The next time it happened, I was the one going deep. I was in Bimini co-leading the wild dolphin swim I previously mentioned.

The first day on the boat, we had a snorkel lesson. Then we went out into open water looking for dolphins.

When we finally found them, our encounter lasted almost an hour. According to the dolphin trip professionals we were working with, that was highly unusual. It was also completely exhausting.

Typically someone on board spots a dolphin fin. The boat captain takes the boat as close as is legally acceptable, and then everyone gets in the water as fast as they can with their snorkel gear on. You swim around for a few minutes with the dolphins and then they are off. Five to ten minutes is about all you get.

I don't know if you have ever been swimming, snorkeling, or diving in open ocean. It is typically very quiet under water. When dolphins are present, boy how things change. Clicks and sounds come from everywhere. It sounds and feels very wild indeed.

Every group (pod) of dolphins is different. Some will come to you as you float around on top of the water. But the Bimini dolphins want you to dive and spin with them. So there you are swimming around in open water. You take the biggest breath you can and then dive down as far as you can go spinning all the while. It's very physically demanding.

With a 45 minute encounter, we were diving and spinning for a very long time.

I trust each person there had at least one moment while the dolphins were present that they will never forget. I know I certainly did.

Going down spinning as far as I could, I had stopped at the bottom of my dive and just sort of hung there in the water. A dolphin came about two feet from me. It seemed to stop as well. Everything suddenly felt very surreal. It was as if time slowed down significantly. We just stayed there gazing at one another for what felt like an eternity. I was no longer hearing clicks or other sounds. Eventually, it was time for me to surface and take a breath. The moment was now over.

It was a fabulous encounter. The tour company said they had never had one last that long.

Good thing we had a great one the first day because we never saw them again the whole week we were there. The sea was very rough. We didn't even go out in the boat a couple of days.

One of the days we didn't go out, I was guided not to go on the hike with the group, but to retire to my room.

Next thing I knew, I was out cold. I was so deep (I assume in Delta) and far out of my body that I could not have roused myself and moved even if the room had been on fire. I was aware of my body so I wasn't asleep. It felt like concrete and like it weighed a ton. I stayed that way for about an hour.

Then, just as my friend had done, I sat bolt upright and knew I had to go to the beach immediately.

It was only a short walk to the beach from my room. I was the only one there.

The beach in Bimini that you see in the image was completely deserted. It was just me with the white sand and the turquoise water.

I felt compelled to get in. I began singing the Language of

Light and saying out loud the statements that came to me. I have never been able to remember what I said. It was information that came through (channeled) in the moment and anchored into my energy field by the beautiful sea. I received a great deal of energy and information during the experience.

Periodically I would get nervous and think about how it's considered unsafe to swim in the ocean alone. I'd get out and walk the beach. Then I would realize how silly I was being.

Obviously, I had been guided to be there. Wasn't I aroused from a deep meditation and practically ordered to go there? Who gets to enjoy a beach this gorgeous all by themselves unless the Universe is making it happen? So I'd get back in again.

After about an hour, one of the islanders showed up. My tranquil moment was over. Its magnificence ever etched in my heart and mind.

The Awakened Brain

There is another brainwave state. It is often referred to as The Awakened Brain. People experiencing peak performance, yogi's, healers, and certain meditators, have a brain wave pattern that is quite different from "normal." Research shows that some dowsers experience this state while using a pendulum. At least one informal set of studies indicates that it sometimes happens in the presence of dolphins.

The individuals experiencing this brainwave state are "firing" in multiple areas of the brain and with simultaneous activity in beta, alpha, theta, and delta. They are accessing Higher Wisdom (receiving inspiration) while being fully conscious and actively talking or questioning (if dowsing). You've never felt so "on" as you do in this state.

I've never been tested for an awakened brain. However, I do often click into what some refer to as "the zone." It happens when

I'm working with clients, speaking, writing, dowsing, and at other times as well.

I believe that the longer you practice a daily meditation, the more likely you are to achieve an Awakened Brain. And even if you don't, if you stick with a meditation practice long enough you will begin to feel calmer and less stressed most of the time.

Meditation Styles

"Reading makes a full man, meditation a profound man, discourse a clear man." ~ *Benjamin Franklin*

 # Meditation
Techniques

In the following pages, you will discover many powerful forms of meditation. You will also find step-by-step details about how to perform several of them.

Others, such as Transcendental Meditation™, primordial sound meditation, traditional shamanic journey, tai chi, yoga, the Silva Method™, and the Dances of Universal Peace require further special training or instruction.

For example, you can't experience the Dances of Universal Peace until you show up at an event, are shown how to do the dance and then perform the dance with the other participants. It can be lots of fun and very "moving" on multiple levels.

An average meditation will last about twenty minutes. Ten minutes isn't long enough and forty-five minutes to an hour should be the maximum. My metaphysical mentor, Stuart Wilde, said you should meditate 24 minutes a day ... *one minute for each hour of the day.* If you are using an audio, then the recording directs the length of the meditation. In a guided journey, you go through the whole journey and then you are done.

For a mantra or breathing-type meditation, I like to keep a clock within eyesight and I occasionally open one eye and register how much time is left. You do NOT want to set an alarm or buzzer! You can become very deep and relaxed in meditation. You don't want to jolt yourself out of it. You want to gently return to the waking state with slight body movements like yawning or moving your hands or feet. Often you will feel like gently stretching.

Affirmations and Conscious Manifestation

Regardless of which form you try, deep meditation is a powerful way to begin consciously creating your reality. While in the deepest part of the meditation, visualize the life of your dreams.

What would you be experiencing or doing if you had the life you desire to manifest?
- ❖ What would you be wearing?
- ❖ Who would be with you?
- ❖ Where would you be?
- ❖ What would you hear, see, smell, feel (emotionally), taste, or touch if the scenario you desire were real?

Once you are clear about what you want, you imagine it as if it is real and happening right now. Get as many senses as possible involved in your imagination. Here are some ideas to get you started. If you want a:
- ❖ Promotion or another form of career success - see people smiling and shaking your hand, patting you on the back, saying "Good job!"
- ❖ New house - imagine yourself getting up in the morning, walking into the kitchen, preparing a cup of coffee and enjoying it in your new home.

❖ Spouse or romantic partner – see yourself in a romantic location holding hands, kissing, or hugging that special someone.

You can also state your affirmation(s), either silently or out loud, before you begin your meditations. Or, conversely, you could say them after.

Affirmations should always be in the present tense as if they are happening right now:

"I have perfect health."

"I have a very satisfying, nurturing relationship."

Be as specific as possible. Saying "I earn more money" is too vague. If you get 1 penny more, that affirmation has been fulfilled!

As I go about my day I often receive flashes of inspiration. One of the things revealed to me in this manner was the best form of communication to choose for manifesting.

Since your intuition is how you receive information from Higher Wisdom, it is also the best way to communicate your desires. Most people's intuition works in one of three ways:

They hear words, sentences, or songs inside their head.

They see flashes of images or little video scenes in their mind's eye.

They feel or "know" things.

If you hear (clairaudient), then the best way to communicate your desires is to state them out loud.

If you see (clairvoyant), then the best way to communicate your desires is to visualize them happening.

If you simply know (clairsentient), then the best way to communicate your desires is to write them down and feel what it would feel like to have your dreams come true. The act of writing is a kinesthetic act. It is a movement that anchors things into the body. That's why I personally take lots of notes when I attend a lecture or watch an instructional video. The act of writing anchors in the information. I almost never have to actually refer to the notes in order to remember the information.

Many people like to do all three.

Mantra Meditation

One of the meditation techniques I use quite often, particularly for creative insights, is a mantra meditation known as *Body Mind Meditation*. You sit quietly for fifteen to twenty minutes repeating silently in your mind a mantra - a series of sounds or words that "charm the mind."

The most popular form of mantra meditation is *Transcendental Meditation*™, also known as TM™. A qualified instructor teaches the person the technique and chooses the particular mantra the person will use. Immediately after doing a mantra meditation, I invariably begin to receive huge creative ideas and my writing just pours forth effortlessly.

TM™ was brought from India to the western world by Maharishi Mahesh Yogi. It became all the rage back in the 60's when the popular band, The Beatles, began doing it. One of Maharishi's most successful students is Deepak Chopra. Deepak ran the Maharishi Ayurvedic Health Center in Lancaster, Massachusetts. Deepak later opened his own center near San Diego, CA where visitors are taught a similar type of meditation to TM™ called *Primordial Sound*.

I was introduced to *Body Mind Meditation* through the Body Mind Center in Reading, PA. My Ayurvedic counselor was Karen Schweitzer, who had been Deepak Chopra's personal assistant at the Center in Lancaster, MA. Her husband, Greg, taught *Transcendental Meditation*™ to all the Center guests, which included many celebrities.

Transcendental Meditation™, *Body Mind Meditation*, and *Primordial Sound Meditation* are taught by trained professionals. During the course of the training, the participant is given a mantra to use.

I highly recommend the *Body Mind Meditation* training for people who want to do a mantra meditation.

However, if you want to get started right away with a mantra meditation, you need a mantra.

A very popular mantra sound is "Om." It represents the Absolute, or God. You say "Ahhhhhhh Uuuuuuuuuuuuuuu Mmmmmmmmmm." And then repeat it again. And then again. And keep that up for fifteen to twenty minutes. The Mmmmm part is almost a hum.

Several gurus suggest, "Om Namah Shivaya." It means I honor my inner or true Self. Each syllable is said very slowly, out loud. The sound of any mantra should create a vibration and feeling within the body.

My good friend, Jonathan Goldman, has a powerful book and workshop on *The Divine Name*. It is a series of sounds invoking God which he "received" through Divine Revelation. After enjoying his workshop one weekend, and toning the sounds suggested, I received another set of sounds for invoking the Divine. I often share those in my workshops.

Sri Swami Satchidananda, founder of Yogaville, suggested that "So Hum" be used along with the breath. As you breathe in you say "Ssssooooooo" and as you breathe out you say "Hhhhhuuuuummm." And you repeat this over and over again in time with the breath. It means "I am He." Or, "I Am that I Am."

Many people choose a powerful word or phrase and use it as their mantra - joy, peace, love, Jesus, I am peace, I am love, etc. Try different ones. They will all work. It is the sound, more than the meaning of the words that act to calm the mind. A really powerful word is Y-E-S-H-U-A. Really sound it out over and over. It calls to the Christ within you.

Sometimes I use the mantra I was given when I was trained eighteen years ago. Other times I use the mantra I "received" directly one day while meditating. Sometimes I do both. I repeat one silently for ten to fifteen minutes followed by the other.

In a mantra meditation, when a stray thought enters the mind, you simply notice and go directly back to repeating the mantra silently. Just recognize that you are "thinking" and go back to thinking the mantra. It is the empty space, the silence between the repetitions of the mantra, where the power lies. In some sessions, you may have many stray thoughts and in others very few. Both are fine. You are meditating perfectly even when you have stray thoughts.

Yantra Meditation

Another way to enhance the mantra meditation is to stare at a geometric pattern instead of having the eyes closed. This is called yantra meditation. Staring also quiets the mind and certain geometric forms trigger deep remembering of your connection with the Divine.

A classic pattern is a circle with a dot in the center. You can easily draw this yourself. Place it somewhere at eye level and repeat a mantra sound or phrase you like. A more complex design to stare at is a mandala. Some people enjoy staring into a fire or a candle flame.

The beautiful images painted by my dear friends Eva Sekmar-Sullivan and Jean-Luc Bozzoli are also fabulous to stare at in meditation.

I love the conversation around the Sri Yantra in the movie the Last Mimzy. It's one of my favorite movies, and I think you will find the references to spirituality and expanded consciousness very compelling.

Breath Awareness

Another version of this is to sit quietly with your eyes closed and just notice your breath. Pay complete attention to your breathing - breathing in, breathing out, breathing in, and breathing out. Concentration on the breath aids in ridding the mind of stray thoughts.

Sounding the Ah

Well known author, Wayne Dyer, made another mantra meditation popular in the western world through his book and audios called *Manifesting Your Destiny*. The guru who taught it to him was Dattatreya Siva Baba. The meditation's purpose is to create the life you choose. According to the teaching, "Ah" is the sound of creation.

Breathe in imagining energy running up your spine and to the top of your head. As you breathe out, you imagine what you want, feel what it would be like to have it, and say "ah" as you imagine energy going straight out your third eye into the universe. Then repeat.

The third eye is the center of the forehead right between the eyebrows where the major nerves of the body meet. Look at picture of a guru from India or a female of the Hindu faith. They often have a bindi on their forehead where the third eye is located.

Take a long inbreath and a long outbreath and the entire time you breathe out you say "aaaaaaahhhhhhh". You do this for six or seven minutes. Then whisper it out loud for six or seven minutes.

Then repeat it in your mind only for six or seven minutes. You have been creating.

There is much more to this meditation of course. Get the book or audios by Dr. Dyer to learn the full technique.

Jonathan Goldman, the friend I mentioned earlier, leads a free global meditation every Valentine's Day (February 14th) called World Sound Healing Day. People from around the world sound Ah at the specified time. Visit his website, http://www.healingsounds.com for details.

Shamanism, Rituals, & Other Practices of Earth-Based Spirituality

According to Sandra Ingerman, renowned shamanism expert and teacher, a shaman is someone who can see in the dark. That means a person who can navigate in the unseen spiritual realms.

Many indigenous cultures have a deep respect and connection with the earth and the natural world. They dance and perform elaborate ceremonies to celebrate life, honor the seasons, and to seek great wisdom.

When the Spanish and other Europeans first encountered the "savages," they considered them ignorant and superstitious. All over the world, they tortured and killed the native people in order to make room for the supposedly superior religion and people of European heritage. The tales of horror are beyond description. Thankfully, they were unable to completely wipe out these cultures.

When one takes the time to look deeper into shamanism and earth-based spirituality, one can find great beauty and wisdom in many of the teachings and ceremonies.

I find it truly fascinating that medical doctors and other health professionals travel in great numbers to Santa Fe to learn shamanic healing. At first glance, that seems pretty shocking. But even the casual observer can see that western medicine does not have all the answers. Shamanism offers a more holistic approach, and soul retrieval and other shamanic healing practices have had great healing success for thousands of years.

Having lived in Northern New Mexico surrounded by the pueblo people for 9 years, I can honestly say that the European invasions, poverty, and alcoholism have taken their toll on these beautiful people. Yet, thankfully, some of their rich heritage remains.

One of the most powerful moments I have ever experienced related to Native American ceremony was one year at Chaco Canyon on Summer Solstice.

Chaco is a remote location in Northern New Mexico with the sprawling remains of an ancient Anasazi (ancient ones) culture. Like many sacred sites around the globe that were designed specifically to align with significant astronomical events. On Summer Solstice at Chaco Canyon, the sun shines through a window in one of the stone walls illuminating another location within. Summer Solstice is the only day this happens. Like Chichen Itza in Mexico and numerous other locations, the ancient people honored the turning of the seasonal wheel. And they did it with astonishing astronomical precision.

Raven and I decided to bring a group there to camp and join up with another group led by our friend, Allison Rae. I sent out an invitation to my growing email newsletter list, and we had people come from all over the U.S. and as far away as Canada to join us there.

Now, after the fact, I laughingly say that no one in their right mind goes to Chaco Canyon for Summer Solstice. It was brutally hot. So hot in fact, that we spent the afternoons sitting in the caves on the side of a cliff. It was simply too hot to walk around or do anything else. There was no shade anywhere.

At noon on the Summer Solstice, Zuni dancers were there to perform a few sacred dances. I had previously seen many dances at the local pueblos near where I lived. And at many events in Santa Fe, a group of Aztec dancers with their giant feather headdresses would perform.

I was not expecting this experience, however.

Chaco had been off limits to the natives for hundreds of years. No-one had been allowed to dance there in ages. It was a great honor for the Zuni to be given the opportunity. And it was an even greater honor for those of us who got to witness.

My friends and I sat cross-legged on the ground in front of the other observers at the edge of the dance space. The singer for the group acted as their spokesperson. A singer is someone who plays the drum and chants or sings the sacred songs that accompany the dancers.

It was the singer who explained to us that no one had been allowed to dance there in hundreds of years. He also shared that for his people, the Zuni, being a dancer was something you were born into. Various families in the pueblo performed different functions. His parents were dancers. Their parents were dancers. And the parents before them and so on back as far as you can imagine.

I love dance. For years and years, it was my first love. As a young girl, my biggest dream was to be a dancer on Broadway. The way my training was shaping up, it was a dream that could have been realized. I was the best dancer at the dance studio where I attended. But time and situations have a way of pointing you in a different direction. I can still easily become quite euphoric and go into a meditative / trance state by moving and becoming one with certain forms of music.

Being in the presence of the Zuni dancers was a powerful experience. As the drum beat began and the singer started his song, the dancers came into the dance space and began their moving prayer. The particular dance they were doing had the dancers all standing in one place moving back and forth with the rhythm of the drumbeat.

One of the dancers was positioned right in front of me. If I had reached out my hand, I could have touched his leg. I stared at this legs and feet, completely ignoring all the other dancers. With each beat of the drum, he landed on the opposite foot. And each time this happened, I could literally feel the energy surge through my entire body. The Zuni dancers were literally waking up the earth. I was moved to tears.

The rituals and ceremonies performed by the native people are far from supplication to heathen gods by the ignorant. They are powerful energy techniques that alter things in both the inner and outer worlds.

Vision Quest

Native Americans, and others who practice their spiritual ways, go on vision quests - a time alone in nature done with fasting and with prayer.

A person who chooses to vision quest does so to seek visions and receive answers about their life mission, their special talents and gifts, and which direction to take when faced with critical life choices.

I've never experienced a multi-day vision quest. However, I did participate in a mini version that involved a sweatlodge before sunrise (for purification). Then I was taken to the top of a mountain and left there alone for 12 hours. I received great insight and had a powerful vision that has shaped my life from that moment forward.

Caution: Never go out into the wilderness and stay alone fasting for several days without being properly prepared and without having someone trained to do this hold the space for you. Every culture I've ever heard of prepares the "initiate" or "quester" with days, weeks, or even years of physical, mental, and emotional preparation. And when the time comes, there is an individual or group of people who "hold the energy" for your vision and your safety. Usually, there is a person with the ability to "track" you. Meaning they can go into meditation and see how you are doing – literally observing you from where they are.

Usui, the founder of the hands-on-healing form known as Reiki, is reported to have spent 21 days on a mountain and "received" the energy and symbols he then taught about and shared in his Usui Reiki Ryōhō Gakkai ~ Usui's Spiritual Energy Therapy Society. The Usui Reiki Ryoho Gakkai, in its original form, is reported to still be practiced within a secret society in Japan.

Many "inspired" creations came from people who were meditating or in a meditative state. This includes great symphonies, art, literature, and invention.

Spending only a few minutes alone in nature can do wonders. I highly recommend it. Take the afternoon. Go on a hike. Find a lovely place to sit. And enjoy one of the meditations described here. One of my favorite spots is near a stream or the ocean. The sound easily transports you into the alpha state.

Herbal Assistance

What I'm talking about are hallucinogenic and other plants or substances used to elicit an altered state of consciousness.

One word sums up my opinion of the matter:

"Don't."

In many indigenous cultures, mind-altering substances of varying degrees of potency and effectiveness have been used for many centuries. Things like ayahuasca, peyote buttons, certain mushrooms, and other herbs are part of their spiritual/religious practice. The shaman (medicine person, spiritual leader) ingests the plant, by whatever method is customary, and is able to access information and experience alternate realities seeking healing or wisdom for the person or group they are assisting.

People seeking alternate states of reality (a "trip" of some kind) have tried using these plants as well as other substances, even LSD. Like a few other indigenous spiritual practices, when one is unprepared for such an experience, disaster and even death can follow. I liken it to giving a hand grenade to a four-year-old. If they figure out how to use it, they can cause irreparable harm to themselves and others.

The meditation forms I'm sharing are safe and beneficial. If you follow the guidelines in *Peering Through the Veil*, you won't need to do anything potentially harmful in order to have extraordinary visions, dreams, and alternate reality experiences.

The purpose of the meditational techniques I am sharing with you is not so you can have some grand vision or psychedelic trip. However, many people experience very vivid imagery and wildly fascinating experiences by performing many of the meditation methods. I have personally had many interesting and intense adventures ~ all from the comfort of my own chair and without the need for mind-altering drugs.

There are people whom I know and trust that have experienced various substances as part of their meditation exploration. Some of these individuals report positive results, particularly for those who are locked into a left-brained skeptical mindset. Based on their experiences and what they have observed in others, they believe a doorway in consciousness can be opened.

Again, I have no experience in this area and therefore suggest great caution if you feel drawn to explore meditation in this way.

Medicine Wheels

A powerful way to enhance meditation is to work with a medicine wheel - another tool from earth-based spirituality, or native cultures. I've had several wonderful experiences while doing guided meditation, transcendental-type meditation, or any number of other forms of meditation while sitting within a medicine wheel circle.

I once had a cat named Smokey that would only come near me if I was asleep or if I was meditating inside a medicine wheel.

Famous author, Barbara Hand Clow, says we have the ability to access 12 dimensions simultaneously when meditating inside a medicine wheel.

We used to have two on our property in New Mexico. Using dowsing tools like L-rods or pendulums, you can read the energy of the medicine wheel. Most spin like a huge vortex.

When we held a pendulum over the sweatlodge or one of the medicine wheels, the pendulum would begin to swing in a large circle. Outside the wheel, the pendulum would be still. Inside the wheel, it would spin.

Building your wheel can be as simple or elaborate as you desire. The simplest medicine wheel is created with four stones. They can be huge rocks that you place permanently in your yard. Or it can be four tiny ones (even crystals) that you carry with you and build the wheel wherever you are.

For an outside wheel, sketch a circle out on the ground with an eight or nine-foot diameter – or any size that is convenient for your space and purpose. It doesn't have to be perfect. You can place a large stone in the center. Then take a 4 to 4 1/2 foot string or rope from the center to the outside to measure and create your eight or nine-foot wheel.

With a compass or GPS system, place each of the four stones on the circle in the directions north, south, east, and west. Enter the circle and ask the energies of those directions to be present. You can also place two stones in the center, one for mother earth, the other for father sky.

A more traditional wheel contains eight stones around the outside. One in each of the directions plus 1 in between each direction (it's a better-defined circle.) This can also be done with twelve stones – one for each direction and two in between each direction.

My favorite book about this topic is *Dancing With the Wheel* by Sun Bear and Wabun Wind. You can learn more about that book, along with several others, in the *Resources* section at the back of this book.

My first meditation with a medicine wheel was a powerful and transformational experience. You read a little about it in *Chapter 2*.

I had purchased the *Dancing with the Wheel* book mentioned above and couldn't wait to build my own personal wheel. The second bedroom in my apartment had been converted into a meditation room. I decided to lay out a medicine wheel on the floor in there, taking up the entire space of the room.

Following the instructions in the book, I visited numerous New Age bookstores and several lapidary shows in order to purchase the crystals necessary to make one of the crystal wheels the book mentions.

Once I had all the stones necessary, I held up each stone and read aloud its purpose in the wheel. I then placed it in its proper position on the floor. It was a very elaborate wheel using many stones and this dedication process took awhile. By the time I was done, the whole room was vibrating with the energy.

I played *Sacred Earth Drums* by David and Steve Gordon as background music. I love this recording for meditations like this.

I then began doing one of the guided meditations the book describes where you pretend you are walking in nature and come upon an ancient medicine wheel. In your mind, you walk around the wheel, stopping at each of the four directions to commune with the animal spirit of that direction. I was overwhelmed with the intensity of the encounters. The animals seemed so real, as if I could touch them. I was not expected it to be nearly that multi-sensory.

Like I mentioned in Chapter 2, while visualizing a coyote inside a medicine wheel, the coyote magically morphed into a dolphin.

I can't explain how or why the dolphins came to me. It is simply what happened. They are the angels of the sea and the messengers of the Divine Feminine. Their presence changed my life and it all began with a medicine wheel.

If you create your own, then keep the space sacred. Only use

the area containing the wheel for prayer, meditation, and healing.

Many people use small crystals, like those in the image, to create their medicine wheels. They carry them in a scarf or bag. The wheel can then be set up in a hotel room, outside, or anywhere they go. It becomes a traveling sanctuary. Anything done or said there has great power.

Individuals who practice Wicca often "cast a circle." That is not my path, so I know very little about it. If I were a person drawn to that form of spirituality, I believe I would start by reading books published through Llewellyn. They have been at it for a very long time and their titles tend to be actively geared toward that.

Regardless of the type of meditation you are doing, I highly recommend doing it inside a medicine wheel.

Sweatlodge

Many people who feel drawn to Native American, or earth-based, spirituality, are often intrigued by the idea of a sweatlodge.

It is not for the faint of heart. It is also not intended as a novelty for the spiritually curious.

If a person is "called" to experience it, then it can be life changing. If they are not, it can literally be life threatening. Many gain something from the experience.

A sweatlodge is a powerful "place" of prayer. The power, intensity, and richness of the experience depends on many factors including the facilitator, the location, how the lodge is set up and dedicated, the other attendees, as well as your physical, mental, and emotional state going into it.

The sweatlodge is an ancient tradition practiced by indigenous cultures from all around the world. The particulars change from culture to culture, but the basis is the same: sweat your ass off so you can know God. *(I know it seems disrespectful or irreverent to describe it this way. Yet it is a highly accurate description.)*

Becoming almost delirious from the heat, participants can access aspects of their subconscious mind and receive insights that they have trouble accessing in normal waking reality.

According to Marsha Scarbrough, author of *Medicine Dance*, "They can release unwanted patterns to be vaporized by the rocks. They can learn to be with fears triggered by the heat, the darkness, the claustrophobia. They can reassemble their molecules into new patterns. Their self-esteem is raised by enduring the difficult challenge."

It typically occurs inside a low round igloo shaped structure that sits on bare earth covered in layer upon layer of blankets. A depression, or pit, is in the center. The lodge is set up very much like a medicine wheel with a domed roof. As I mentioned earlier, a pendulum will spin over a lodge. That is because, like a medicine wheel, it creates a dimensional portal.

Participants crawl in one at a time and sit facing the center. Lava rocks are heated for hours in a fire and are then brought in one by one to the center of the lodge carried on pitchforks (outside the lodge) and deer antlers (inside the lodge). When enough rocks are in the pit, the door flap is closed.

Inside it is completely dark. You can't see your own hand. If the rocks are hot enough, you can see them glowing red for a little while.

The lodge leader takes a ladle and pours water on the rocks. They crackle and fizz while steam billows up engulfing the participants. The leader then ladles more water on the rocks, creating even more steam and heat.

Sitting in complete darkness, sweat pouring off of you, the air so thick with steam that the nostrils are burning with heat, and now it's time to pray.

Each lodge is a bit different, but it can include the leader singing native songs either alone or with the participants, he or she will give instructions about the intent of this "round," she or he will offer a prayer, each participant is given an opportunity to pray out loud one at a time or they are asked to do it in silence. People often see visions and experience great insight. Some receive healing.

If the prayers/chants/meditations are out loud, the number of participants and how much they each say will determine the length of the round.

When the first round is over, the door flap is opened. Light enters along with refreshing cool air providing a brief respite from the intense heat.

Sometimes "newbies" bail after the first round. In some lodges, that is completely fine. In others, you are expected to stay in the entire time.

The door flap isn't opened to let in fresh air. The door is opened to allow the energies that have been released inside to be set free out into the Universe. It is also opened to bring in more heated lava rocks in preparation for round two. When enough rocks have been added to the pit, the door is again closed, darkness once again descends, water is again ladled, and prayers are again given. If you thought round one was hot, well guess what? Round two is often hotter.

This typically continues for four rounds. The lodges I've encountered vary in length from 1 to 3 hours.

I find enduring a sweatlodge more physically challenging than giving birth. And I'm not exaggerating when I say that. Of course, my experience of giving birth wasn't that difficult, and I was in a meditational trance state much of the time. I had Jess in a pool of water at home with only Raven present. It took six hours from the first barely noticeable contractions to his entrance into the world.

I think the first lodge is probably the hardest. Until you have sat in one, it is hard to imagine what it is actually like ~ a bit like having your first child. You can talk about it all day long. But until you have actually been there, you can't possibly really understand.

Can you remember a time when you were in a really hot and humid place and sweating a lot? In those situations, I find I don't want my arm to touch my side or for my legs to touch one another because it seems to feel even hotter and stickier when they do.

The thing I found most interesting in my first lodge was the realization that it didn't matter if my arm was on my leg. It was so hot in the space, that the temperature of my body parts did not make any difference whatsoever.

I've also never sweated so much. There is so much steam and so much sweat that no matter what you are wearing, it is completely soaked and dripping by the end of the lodge.

The other amazing thing is that a person's body can tolerate that much heat. While you are in there, particularly the first time, you ponder how that is even possible.

At the end of my first lodge, we all crawled out and then everyone simply collapsed on the ground and napped for about half an hour.

I haven't done a sweat lodge in many years. Once again, I only recommend it to those who truly feel the calling to do so.

There are people who receive a great deal of benefit from the lodge experience. They feel renewed and refreshed afterward. They feel their prayers have been heard, and they have been purified body, mind, and soul.

The sweatlodge is a significantly grueling physical experience. People with health issues should not participate without checking it out first with their doctor.

If you feel drawn to do a lodge, find a facilitator that you resonate with. Ask as many questions as possible so you know what to expect. Every facilitator does it their own unique way, based on their inner guidance or their rigorous training.

The clothing expected, or unexpected, can vary wildly depending on the type of lodge and the facilitator. In some traditional lodges, if women are even allowed, they must wear a long skirt. In others, people wear bathing suits or nothing under a sarong and once in the lodge they drop the sarong. If you aren't expecting it, and you certainly can't see what the people around you are doing once the lodge door is closed, it can be quite shocking when the door is opened after the first round to find the guy opposite you has no clothes on. So finding out about expected clothing is a great question to ask.

There are also other questions like are you expected to bring a tobacco offering or other gift for the facilitator and fire tender(s)? Do you need to bring food for the feast afterward? Is a financial donation expected or recommended?

Guided Visualization Meditations

A very popular form of meditation is Guided Meditation or Shamanic Journey. There are thousands of audios available where someone has taken some relaxing music (to put your brain in the alpha state) and spoken over top of the music to guide you through a visualization of places and events which can calm your mind and emotions, allow you to do some physical healing, and to create the future you choose.

Whether you create your own journey, listen to one on audio, or do the one I offer here, it's important to get all your senses involved. See everything in as true a color as possible - a blue sky, a bright yellow flower. Hear what the sounds might be - birds singing, water babbling in a brook. Smell the forest or flowers. Touch the tree. Feel the ground beneath your feet. If there is something to taste, get that sensation also.

You can take yourself on a guided meditation. With each part of the journey, really drink in the scenery and don't forget to use all the senses. Stay in each location, or doing each activity, for as long as it takes to feel real and to get you to feel relaxed.

Don't have expectations of what meditating will be like. Some people get very vivid visuals, others hear sounds, and still others feel things. Each way is correct. Almost no-one does all three.

A Sample Guided Meditation Journey:

This meditation, like all guided meditations, works best if you listen to it rather than try to read it and follow along. It's hard to drop into an alpha or theta brainwave when you are trying to read.

I have recorded this meditation for you in my voice. Visit:
https://www.MagnificentU.com/PeeringMP3.

You can listen to it online or download the audio MP3 file. Before you begin, read over the preparation instructions in Chapter 5.

- Begin by sitting or lying quietly. Close your eyes. Take a few slow deep breaths. Focus your attention on your heart.
- See yourself standing in a field. See the grasses moving in the wind. Feel the wind and the sun on your skin. Take a few moments to really take in this experience.
- Look around and notice all the things in the field.
- At some point, you may see an animal run across the field.
- Notice what kind of animal it is and what it is doing.
- Slowly move your head so that you can take a long slow look at everything in the field.
- Somewhere near the edge of the field, you notice a gate.
- Slowly walk towards the gate.

- What does the gate look like? How high is it? How wide? Is it really ancient or brand new? What is it made of?
- Begin to open the gate.
- How hard is it to open?
- Sense yourself going through the gate. (You may wish to cross a bridge instead of entering a gate - it's only a preference. Just go through the same questions and really feel the bridge. Feel yourself crossing it.)
- How does it feel now that you have gone through the gate or across the bridge?
- You notice a winding path leading into a forest.
- Get on the path and begin to follow it.
- As you near the forest, what do you see? What kinds of trees are there? Is it an evergreen forest with very little undergrowth, or is it a deciduous forest with moss on rocks, and bushes and wildflowers? Do you see any animals?
- Enter the forest. Hear the birds. Look for the various plants and animals that may be present. You may see dwarfs, fantasy animals, or flower devas. Just notice.
- Continue to follow the path through the forest.
- As you follow the path, you will eventually come to a stream or other body of water.
- Spend some time by the water. Hear the water over the rocks. Imagine what it feels like to sit there beside the water. If it's a pond or lake, see a fish jump and hear the splash.
- Now continue on your journey through the forest.
- Up ahead there is a clearing.
- Walk out into the clearing and you will notice a building. What does it look like? Is it wood, brick, stone, big, small, new, or old?

- Walk up to the building and notice the door.
- The door opens for you. Do not worry, it is very safe here.
- You go inside and meet your "guide." Your guide's energy is not one recognized by your brain, so doing the best that it can, it creates an image for you to relate to. It may be a saint, an animal, a dwarf, an angel, a monk, a geometric shape, a ball of light - the possibilities are endless. There is no right or wrong way to see the guide. Just don't get caught up in the image.
- The guide shows you around the building. There is a library inside and the guide takes you through the library to find the answers to any questions you might have.
- You can go to a book, open it, read an answer, and then replace the book. Stay here as long as you like.
- Be sure to thank the guide before you leave.
- Go back towards the path through the woods.
- Walk back the same way you came.
- Soon you see the clearing where the forest meets the meadow.
- Walk back into the meadow.
- As you feel ready, begin to gently wiggle your fingers and toes.
- Move your head around a bit.
- Begin to gently move your arms and legs.
- Remember that you are here in this room.
- When you are completely ready, open your eyes.

Be sure to write notes about your experience.

In some versions of this meditation, you simply ask the guide a question or simply ask for insight and hear or "feel" an answer instead of reading in a book. Try both ways. The more you do the journey, the easier it becomes. Always write down your insights. For many people, the entire journey will be different each time they experience it.

Shamanic Journey

In a traditional Shamanic Journey, the shaman, or person learning shamanic ways, takes a journey to the underworld, middle world or upper world to do healing or whatever their intent is.

Underworld does not mean lower world or hell. It means an inner world, a place where the brainwaves are slower, deeper, an entirely different realm of existence. They enter through a Sipapu (a hole in the ground that is a gateway to another world). This can be a hole, a cave, or some other doorway – even the gate or bridge we crossed in the earlier guided meditation.

Once in this other world, they meet and work with their animal helper or spirit guide. This is the traditional way a shaman works with a person to do soul retrieval and other healing.

Years after I first developed the *Meeting Your Dolphin Guide Meditation,* in my eBook *Dancing with Dolphins*, I took a Shamanic Healers workshop with Sandra Ingerman. I was delighted to discover that going "down" into the ocean is a common way to enter a shamanic journey.

Even though I had not previously had any formal shamanic training, I had been doing it, and teaching it, "right" all along. I received the words to the meditation during a deep trance meditation. In fact, most of my insights come during, or soon after, my morning meditations.

The Silva Method™

Many meditation techniques are based on the visualization and healing work of Jose Silva called the *Silva Technique* or *Silva Method*™.

The weekend workshop I attended was a truly enriching experience. I greatly enjoyed the instructor, Jeanie Bingston, and had so much fun doing all the meditation exercises.

The method contains a series of powerful meditations that literally program your mind for healing, better concentration, doing better in school, having more energy, and improving your sleep. The list of things you can improve using the techniques is virtually endless.

We learned ways to evaluate health issues, drop into alpha at will, and remote view. We also explored communication with plants, minerals, and animals.

It was very empowering and I think it could greatly assist practically anyone wishing to make life improvements. I feel it would be particularly beneficial for teenagers and young adults.

You can now enjoy the power of this method from the convenience of your own home. Everything is now available as home study courses.

Learning the technique is well worth the money. You can go into an alpha state meditation and heal your body, fix your car, heal others, learn to do medical intuitive type activities as popularized by Caroline Myss, talk with your pets, and a whole lot more.

I've seen influences of the Silva technique in everything from an *Alivening Weekend* I took with Glen Smyly to a *Technologies for Creating* course designed by Robert Fritz. You can program your subconscious mind to do extraordinary things. In the Silva class, you aren't just hearing about being able to do wild things with your mind. You are actually doing them.

 # Sound Meditations

I had been meditating for a couple of years when I felt the inner promptings to attend a flower essence weekend workshop with Star Riparetti of *Star Flower Essences*. (The Andean Orchids are simply heaven!)

If I had only known what I was about to get myself into. Looking back now, I have to laugh.

I assumed I was taking the workshop so that I could incorporate *Star Flower Essences* into my work and include them in the products I offered students, clients, and customers.

Boy was I wrong!

I have always had a very special connection with flowers. Even my first snake encounter involves a flower story.

When I was a child, my mom and I stayed in Virginia for several weeks.

Her mother, my grandmother, was dying of bone cancer. My mom was taking care of her, cooking meals and caring for the household. I was a city kid and knew nothing about country living. Here we were in the middle of tobacco farming country. I found myself surrounded by miles and miles of farmland.

My uncle had the farm next door, so my cousins were trying to keep me entertained while mom stayed busy caring for Big Ma, as she was called.

They took me down to the creek to play. We saw a tiny black snake in the water. I thought it was delightful. But both cousins seemed concerned as they looked at each other and said, "You know what that means!" Well, I had no idea what it meant. So they explained that it meant that mom and dad snake were somewhere close by.

Those words would come back to haunt me later.

Like I said before, I have always loved flowers.

On the other side of the road across from my grandparent's farmhouse were tons of wildflowers. The day after we had seen the snake, I decided to pick a beautiful bouquet of flowers for my mom. I was carrying a wonderful selection all delicately arranged and started towards the house to present them. That must have been when I saw the snake.

This event was truly traumatic for me, and I actually can't remember all the details.

I wasn't allowed to go into the house through the front door. My mom is pretty intent on keeping things clean. If I went in through the back door, then I could take off my shoes on the screened in porch and not get any dirt on the floor.

As I made my way around the house to the back door, I encountered the largest black snake anyone has seen around there even to this day. It was literally the entire length of the house.

I simply don't remember how I got past it.

I do remember standing at the back door shaking all over. Apparently, I couldn't open the door, so I had to knock to get in. I stood there shaking, trying to talk, and attempting to give my mom the beautiful flowers I had picked for her. As I held them up, the whole bouquet was shaking.

I did the best I could to get into the house quickly and explain about the snake. I remember trying to speak and all that would come out was, "the the there there's a a b bbig snake."

My grandfather, Papa, got out his shotgun and went outside to confront the snake and take care of the problem. I had never seen a gun before. I had no idea that my grandfather even owned one.

As I looked out the window still shaking, I tried to watch my grandfather kill the snake. Because of the location, I wasn't able to see ~ thankfully. I heard a shot. After a fairly long delay, I heard another.

Across the way on my uncle's farm, my cousin was trying to mount her horse. Each time a shot was fired at the snake, the horse reared, and she was thrown off. The cousin who was with me when we saw the young snake was being thrown off her horse when the big snake was killed. I have always found that very fascinating. I've never figured out the significance. I just feel there is an important connection.

I avoided being alone in nature for quite a while after that. I'm so glad I got over it.

I find every flower precious and unique. I love them all so dearly. It is as if they are my friends. When I look out a window, it is always the little areas of color coming from the flowers that catches my eye. This has always been true even when I was a small child riding in a car.

My parents drove me all over North America to visit the major sights: the Grand Canyon, New York City, the homes of various Presidents, museums, caverns, and all 48 of the continental states. We crossed miles and miles of woodlands, streams, meadows, mountains, and deserts. All along the way, I would notice the little patch of pink or yellow or blue coming from the groups of flowers. It could even be the tiniest hint of color way on the other side of a field. It always caught my eye and brought me joy.

So now I found myself at a weekend workshop with *Star Flower Essences*. I was six months pregnant.

In class, we played with the Andean orchids, learned a great deal about flower essences, and did numerous exercises. The final afternoon we made a flower essence ourselves.

We had been taken to a farm somewhere near Santa Barbara. The class participants were split into two groups. One group was to make a flower essence from Sunflower. The other group, the one I was in, would be working with Nasturtium.

One of our classmates, David Jonas, was quite gifted with flower essences. He had traveled to Australia to study with Ian White and work with the *Australian Bush Essences*. He had also visited Alaska and worked with the essences there. Now he was in Santa Barbara working with *Star Flower Essences*. Since he had already had the opportunity to make essences in these previous workshops, Star asked him if he would hold the bowl as the rest of us cut the flower blooms.

We were instructed to sit and meditate with the plant and to carefully choose which bloom to cut. I didn't really have to do any of that because as soon as she told us what to do, I saw one of the blooms begin to glow. It was completely surrounded by white light. I knew that was the bloom I was to cut.

David carefully held the bowl of water under the bloom as each of our classmates cut the one they had chosen. I was just sure someone else would see the glowing bloom and cut it before I got my turn. I was actually surprised that no-one did.

When it was my turn, I indicated which bloom I was to cut. He held the bowl underneath it. He said that as soon as my bloom hit the water, a rush of energy went through the entire bowl.

Flower essences usually take a few hours in the sun. But according to David, that essence was made the second my bloom hit the water.

David and I became great friends after that. To this day, he is the only person I will let into my laboratory to play around alchemically with my essences, mixing various energies together to create something new.

But the story doesn't end there . . .

I mentioned previously that I was pregnant when I attended the workshop. During the entire pregnancy, I had walked two miles each day through the wildflower meadows on Palomar Mountain in Southern California where I lived. I had been communing with the flowers there for months. Each different type of flower brought me a unique kind of joy.

Upon my return from the workshop, I began waking up almost every morning at 4 a.m. with an image in my mind of one of those wildflowers on Palomar Mountain. I was up and cutting glowing blooms by 6 a.m. each day.

I had no idea that I was going to be making flower essences myself when I attended that workshop.

But then something else happened. During my meditations one day I "got" that I should add sound to the flower essences. And I was given a procedure for doing so.

That made me uncomfortable.

I knew a lot about energy healing. I'd studied chakras, crystals, healing meditations, and various energy healing methods. But I knew nothing about sound healing and I felt unprepared to tell people that "hey, these are great because I've added sound."

I felt like I needed a credible sound healer's blessing. So I went online in search of sound healing and sound healers. I visited numerous websites. The one that stuck out was Jonathan Goldman's *Healing Sounds* website. Everything I read there strongly resonated with me.

I contacted him. We emailed back and forth numerous times as he patiently answered my questions about sound healing. Eventually, I gave him a call sharing with him about the flower essences that I was creating and the process I'd been given to infuse them with sacred sound. He got quiet for a moment as he communicated with Archangel Shamael (Metatron) about what I'd said, and responded that "Yes, indeed, that would work."

Yeah. I had confirmation from a leader in the field!

Jonathan and I finally met in person at the International New Age Trade Show in Denver. I've been close friends with he and his lovely wife, Andi, ever since. It has been such a great honor to infuse his music into essence form. We call the collaboration, *The Essence of Sound.*

As you sample the smorgasbord of meditation I am sharing with you in this book, be sure to include sound healing.

As you intone the sounds while chanting, the vibrations do extraordinary things to your body. They greatly assist in aligning body, mind, and soul. Sound is particularly beneficial for shifting your emotional state.

I told you how sounding the mantra in your mind sets up a vibration within your body and that it is the sound that charms the mind. Chanting takes this to a whole new level. Humming is a very beneficial and healthy practice. Andi and Jonathan recently came out with a new book dedicated exclusively to the healing power of humming.

I don't think I've ever met an unhappy person who hums. Think about that.

Whether you chant an ancient Tibetan chant, or you just tone a single note out loud, sound can be a powerful thing.

Make a sound with a single note, like blowing a flute or horn without changing the finger positions. Then try going higher and lower on the scale, and playing around with how loud you make the sound.

Toning with others is extremely uplifting. It's fun to hear your own voice. It's even more fun to have a group of people toning, each using their own sound, eventually harmonizing and moving together in waves of sound.

When I close my eyes, chanting or toning alone or with a group, I often see images within my mind's eye. It can be highly entertaining.

I strongly recommend Jonathan Goldman's various chanting CDs. *Chakra Chants*, *Ultimate Om*, and *The Lost Chord* are wonderful to listen to while in meditation. This image is of me with Andi and Jonathan Goldman at one of their workshops.

His book, CD, and workshop about *The Divine Name* show you an extremely empowering way to make sound. It realigns things so effectively, that just intoning the sounds once or twice and you can actually feel giddy and almost tipsy.

I showed Jess how to do it one day. He joked afterward and said, "Why would anyone do drugs when you can feel like this with just your voice?"

Happiness through sound.

Audio Brainwave Entrainment

Much has changed since I first began meditating. Articles about it are now included in such mainstream magazines as *Shape* and even *Newsweek*. It has become quite commonplace.

Even though not everyone has tried it, many have at least heard of it. Along with yoga, meditation has definitely hit the mainstream.

With popularity comes more scientific ways of meditating. Brainwave research has allowed audio manufacturers to create ways to reach deeper states of mind with very little effort.

Many companies offer brainwave entrainment audio programs. To "entrain" the brain means to cause the brainwaves to match a frequency being sent to it.

Brainwave entrainment works much like tuning forks. Tuning forks are precision cut metal rods with two prongs used to tune musical instruments. When a tuning fork is tapped on a hard surface, the prongs begin to vibrate and give off a particular perfectly pitched tone.

If one tuning fork is already toning, and you hold it next to another one cut for the same pitch, the second one will begin to tone even if you don't touch the two or tap the second. It simply begins to resonate or entrain with the first one.

When you work with brainwave entrainment software or audios, the frequencies sent out as sound, typically through headphones, cause the brain to entrain and slow down to the particular frequency of the sound. There are various types of entrainment audios. The three primary forms are monaural beats, binaural beats, and isochronic tones.

Monaural Beats

A monaural beat is a single sound repeated at specific intervals. The brain gets in sync with the sound and slows down to the rhythm of the tone. Rattles, single drum beats, and metronomes are examples of monaural beats.

The rattles and drums used in shamanic journeys fall into this category. They greatly assist in slowing down the brainwaves to a specific level.

One of my favorite early teachers was Stuart Wilde. Stuart's method of meditation, at the time, was a theta meditation using a metronome sound that slows your brainwave down to the theta level. It's a very deep meditation. Stray thoughts rarely occur because the metronome so charms the mind. After prolonged use, the metronome is no longer needed, and this brainwave can even be sustained with the eyes open. With the metronome you can do a guided meditation or not, it's up to you. He later began offering audio meditations for alpha, theta, and delta.

After working with Stuart's theta meditations for a period of about three years, I developed the ability to move into a theta state. I can even hold that brainwave state with my eyes open.

When you "click into" theta, it is extremely easy to disconnect from your emotions and remain calm, centered, and focused whenever the need arises. It allows me to dowse without involving my desires, beliefs, or emotions to sway the answers.

It allowed me to remain in a trance state when I gave birth to my son at home in water with only Raven present.

It allows me to not freak out when things go awry or when split-second decisions are required.

On more than one occasion I have avoided an auto collision because I am very aware of everything going on simultaneously around me. And I have the ability to act instantly when things are not "right."

As a car or truck suddenly comes out of nowhere or swerves into my lane, I can immediately slam on brakes and blast the horn at the same time. Passengers who are fortunate, or unfortunate (haha), to be riding with me at the time often look over and ask, "How did you do that?" It's just how I'm wired because of all the meditation in theta and the ability to click into "the zone."

When I was first learning to meditate, in addition to doing my daily transcendental-type meditation each morning, I often used the guided meditations and theta metronome sounds by Stuart Wilde. I still enjoy them. They are hard to come by, but definitely worth it. Even though hearing the beeps can be a bit annoying, the audios are very effective, and you don't have to wonder what's happening below your hearing threshold.

I try to steer clear of subliminal audios unless all the words being used are fully disclosed. And, I insist that those words fit into what I consider "good" for programming the subconscious mind.

Conscious language is very important. What you tell your subconscious mind is critical to your health, well-being, level of consciousness and so forth. Visit this link to read more about the conscious use of language in an article I wrote about the subject: https://www.MagnificentU.com/Words.

Binaural Beats

Binaural beats is a very popular technology for brainwave entrainment. Signals are sent to each ear through headphones. The two sounds are not identical but are specifically spaced apart forcing the brain to hear what seems to be a 3rd sound or beat. The beat is actually not there but is created by the brain itself. Proponents of this technology say that it causes breakthroughs for many individuals in mental ability, focus, concentration, creativity, and much more.

The Monroe Institute puts out numerous audio CD's called Hemi-Sync that use binaural beat technology. They have years of research backing up their technology, and from what I can tell, good results. A few of Jonathan Goldman's CDs also contain binaural beat technology.

I tried a very popular, and rather expensive, audio technology program that uses binaural beats to help you reach deep meditative states. The binaural beats were masked by the sound of rain. Unfortunately, being a clairsentient *(one who feels everything)*, I entrained to delta with the sound of rain. So, after using that program for only a short period of time, the minute it started to rain, my body began shutting down and my brain dropped down into a deep delta meditative state.

That is very dangerous when driving a car. I'm not talking about listening to the audio while driving. I'm talking about my body automatically going into a significantly slower brainwave pattern whenever it started to rain.

Obviously, I no longer use those audios. It took a year or two to finally get straightened out and no longer go practically unconscious whenever it rained. I've been a bit more cautious about binaural beat technology in delta ever since.

For eons, humans have been using meditation to slow down their brainwaves and achieve these levels. Now, with technology, there are ways to access the levels faster with less effort. Sometimes technology is a good thing. Other times it is not ~ like my example above.

There are many success stories concerning the use of binaural beats for alpha and theta brain waves. The benefits that happen in alpha and theta have been studied for a long time. Our minds naturally go through these levels as we are falling asleep or are asleep. And it is naturally where our brainwaves go when we meditate.

Gamma, on the other hand, is a much newer animal. It is only now beginning to be discussed in the more mainstream venues. It has had much less scientific research. And yet, various companies are making binaural beat audio files available for you to force your brain to produce more gamma waves. I think this is a very bad idea! And visiting various online forums, I've seen some people talking about very unpleasant side effects that they are experiencing and can only hope will disappear with more use of the technology.

The brain is nothing to play around with. Who knows, over prolonged use, if these people will experience improvements in their life, or if they might experience permanent brain damage?

The techniques I am teaching you in this book have been used successfully for many years with only positive side effects. Do not be tempted to short cut them with unproven technology that could actually be dangerous.

I've listed a few that I enjoy in the *Resources* section at the back.

Isochronic Tones

One of the newer technologies is Isochronic Tones. It is similar to monaural beats in that it only emits one tone at specific intervals. It works a bit differently though, because unlike monaural beats, it works well even without headphones.

I've tried several isochronic tone programs and, so far, I really enjoy the result.

I Still Choose Theta

Early on I was using Stuart Wilde's Theta Meditation exercises. Even though I've done many other forms, for lots of reasons I continue to return to various forms of theta meditation. As I've experienced personally, and as several other researchers have concluded, it is the most effective for healing and personal transformation.

It took me ten years to find the "right" theta brainwave entrainment music to put behind my voice for guided meditations. I've created an entire Magnificent U Meditation Program using these powerful tones to gently guide your brain into a theta brainwave while I take you on several shamanic journeys. The various meditations are for healing, insight, meeting a spirit guide, even traveling to other realms. I've made two of the audios from this program available to you for free. Just visit this link to download them and experience guided meditations, shamanic journey, and brainwave entrainment all at the same time.

Moving
Meditations

Meditations while moving can also be very powerful. Various techniques exist to center the mind and body while moving.

Tai Chi

Tai Chi and Chi Kung are great examples. After learning the form, you practice it once or twice a day as a profound tool for getting in touch with and strengthening the body, connecting with nature as you stand on mother earth, going into the breath and presenting your body movement as a prayer.

Repetitive practice of Tai Chi has the powerful effect of meditation plus strengthening the body and developing personal power. The Tai Chi and Chi Kung movements also open up the energy channels in the body, allowing energy and information to more easily flow.

Tiger Walking

Another moving meditation is Tiger Walking. It's an oriental technique of stepping by landing on the outside of the foot, rolling to the ball and toes, and finally dropping the heel. It's a very graceful walk that requires complete concentration. Balance is easily lost. I first heard about it from Stuart Wilde.

I believe Tiger Walking is what they were trying to show you on the old television show called Kung Fu. The young initiate had to walk across the rice paper without tearing it. I've done this in the forest and on the beach. So much effort goes into the movement that the brain slows down, stray thoughts don't occur, and deep mind is reached.

Yoga

Yoga practiced on your own as a technique to get deeply in touch with your body, to center the mind, and as prayer has a deeply healing effect. The body stores trauma and emotion. Yoga triggers the release of emotional memory locked in the cells

similar to what is available through hands on healing, massage, acupuncture/acupressure, etc.

Yoga has even been known to trigger past life memory. One of my favorite books is *Initiation* by Elizabeth Heich. It is the story of how yoga unlocked an extremely interesting past life memory of her being an initiate in Egypt.

This image shows a person standing in what is called the "tree pose." It is very calming and centering. It's a bit difficult for people who don't' have good balance.

The Sun Salute is probably the most well known, and often practiced, yoga movement series. It stretches, moves, and wakes up the entire body. It opens up all the energy channels and centers within your body. It is one of my favorite ways to start the day.

Fire Walking

Firewalking is another indigenous ritual practiced for thousands of years around the globe. It was made popular by personal development trainers who use it to assist participants in gaining courage and confidence.

I've only attended one firewalk and I had not intended to participate in that one. The Universe had other plans.

Some people think about walking on fire and say "So what?" because it is no big deal. Others think it's nuts - not being able to imagine doing it and wondering why anyone would want to.

I always fell into the first category. When I first heard about firewalking, I knew it was something I could do with little to no effort and certainly no cause for getting all bent out of shape about. So I never intended to do it. I had nothing to prove and it didn't feel like some challenge I needed to overcome.

I found myself firewalking anyway.

Raven, Jess, and I were visiting southern California when Jess was just over a year old. We lived in Canada at the time. It was a 4-day camping event led by our good friend, Happy Bear, where they were doing both sweat lodges and fire walks.

There was a seminar in the afternoon for the people planning to fire walk that night. It prepared them physically and mentally. They did exercises that pushed the boundaries of what is and isn't possible ... *getting the mind and body ready*.

The facilitator had them perform several exercises to build confidence. In one exercise, two participants faced one another with the end of a fairly thick piece of rebar placed horizontally between them at their throat. At the appointed time, they each stepped forward bending the rebar. It reminded me of a team of football players getting all psyched up before a game.

I didn't participate in any of that. I wasn't going to fire walk and I was caring for a 1-year old. I decided to take a nap instead.

When they were ready to actually do the fire walk, Raven came to get me. He suggested I come out to support those who were doing it and hold the energetic space for that to happen.

All of the participants took their turn at walking across the red hot embers. When it was Raven's turn, he took Jess out of my arms and carried him across the fire. I watched as each person took their turn walking across the glowing embers. Two guys with African drums (djembes) walked, almost danced, while drumming.

After they had each had a turn to walk for themselves and their own empowerment, Happy Bear announced that it was now time to walk for others or for a cause. It was then that I knew I had to walk. When you are called, you are called. When you know, you simply know.

So I took off my shoes, handed my baby to Raven, and stood before the field of burning embers.

I looked up into the heavens and said, "I walk for all my sisters who need to be empowered"

I was walking for:

- my sisters of every shape, color, size, religion, age, nationality, political view, sexual preference, income, and education level,
- my sisters being treated like second class citizens,
- my sisters without the means to care for themselves or their children,
- my sisters being sexually abused and abandoned by their families or their tribe,
- my sisters in abusive marriages and other harsh situations,

- my sisters who are homeless,
- my sisters who are jobless,
- my sisters who believe themselves to be less than, to be unworthy of receiving what they desire, to be unlovable,
- my sisters who don't feel beautiful because they feel too thin, too fat, too old, too young, too this, too that, too something, and fail to see their own magnificence,
- my sisters everywhere who could find such happiness and joy if they had even a glimmer of how they are viewed in God's eyes,
- my sisters.

No prep. No plan to do it. No fear. As my brain clicked effortlessly into a trance state, I walked with confidence, trust, and love in my heart. I felt nothing - not even the tiniest amount of heat. No pain. No blisters. Just the knowing that I did what I was called to do.

Many people went to bed with blisters that night.

I didn't do it to empower myself, I did it to empower others. I didn't do it to prove to myself that I could. I did it because I knew in my heart that I was being called (asked) to do so.

Trance Dance

Trance Dance is free-form dancing to "trance dance" type music. Gabrielle Roth is one of the early pioneers. Just let the music move your body any way it wants to.

I suggest having the lights low. Clear a space to move. Let your eyes softly gaze at the ground only enough to make sure you don't run into anything. Concentrate on how your body feels while it's moving.

I used to teach a workshop called *Awakening the Dolphin Within*. One of the activities I had participants do was what I called the

Dolphin Dance. I'd lower the lights and play soft music with dolphin sounds. I showed the participants how I typically danced to such music, moving my body and arms gracefully like I was moving through water, and then I encouraged them to join in.

It usually takes three to five minutes for everyone to get over being self-conscious. After that, things get really interesting and truly beautiful to behold. It is so moving to watch someone express themselves through dance.

I highly encourage you to try it for yourself.

Dances of Universal Peace

Other "body prayers" include *Dances of Universal Peace* where a circle, or many circles, are formed and dancers perform precise dances and sing chants that awaken deep memory of connection with earth and other humans. A profound state of bliss can be achieved.

My first experience of the *Dances of Universal Peace* happened unexpectedly.

It was around 1995. I had just reawakened to spirituality. I was seeing Karen Schweitzer frequently and had been reading all of Stuart Wilde's material. One of the things I learned quickly was to pay attention to my intuition.

As I visited various New Age bookstores, I found that sometimes when I read the name of a book, I would get tears in my eyes. This was my signal that I was supposed to purchase and read it.

Some New Age bookstores and health food stores have free magazines with articles and advertising from local people and organizations offering classes, products, and services. It was through one of those that I found Karen. It was also through one of those that I saw an ad for a *Desert Wisdom Weekend* with Neil Douglas Klotz.

At the time, I was feeling very drawn to the American Southwest and Native American spirituality. I had already built the medicine wheel in my 2nd bedroom and dolphins were already joining me in practically every meditation.

When I saw the ad and got tears in my eyes, I thought it was a workshop about the Southwestern American desert and the native pueblos there.

I had an inner knowing that I was supposed to attend the weekend. It made me very uncomfortable. I knew nothing about it. I knew no-one involved. I'd never heard of Neil Douglas Klotz. It was way out of my comfort zone. But, I knew I was being led there, so I wasn't going to let my discomfort stop me.

Sometimes early on when my intuition inspired me to do something that I would rather not do, I would somehow manage to convince myself that taking an action, like asking a question or making a phone call, would get me off the hook. I tried to logic myself into believing that by making the phone call I was following my intuition. But I convinced myself that when I made the phone call, the workshop would already be filled and I wouldn't have to actually do the thing I didn't want to do.

Funny how it never really turned out that way.

I called the number on the ad and said, "I'm sure your *Desert Wisdom Weekend* is full already. Right?" The response was, "Oh, no, we have plenty of room."

Yikes!

I began asking questions about what the weekend was about. Neil Douglas Klotz was apparently some internationally famous guy and people were flying in from everywhere to do this weekend event with him. It wasn't about the desert in the American Southwest. It was about the Middle East. There would be live musicians, vegan food, and dancing all weekend long.

"O.K. then, sign me up."

To say I was nervous would barely cover it.

The event was held at a lovely retreat in eastern Pennsylvania. I felt completely like a fish out of water. I was the only woman there wearing makeup. All the other ladies were in beautiful flowing skirts and Birkenstock-type sandals. When you are used to four and five-star resorts, sleeping in a room full of cots with a bunch of women that you don't know seems a bit like Mars. I had to ask someone what hummus was. The vegan dishes were marvelous, but I'd never heard of any of them.

Neil's ability to create sacred space was truly amazing. He had recently written a book called *Desert Wisdom,* and this was the workshop associated with that. He taught us sacred Middle Eastern chants and dances that we performed for hours. The music played by live musicians significantly added to the depth of the experience. I told you earlier how much I loved dancing. This was a completely euphoric experience.

I truly loved singing in a foreign language. I speak the Language of Light (a.k.a. Speaking in Tongues), so it wasn't that foreign a concept. I liked it because I didn't have to think about the words, I could simply feel how they made me feel when I sang them and danced the particular dance.

We did a meditation one afternoon and once again I merged with all things. I discuss the first time that happened in another chapter. It was an extremely powerful experience.

At the end of the weekend, I purchased Neil's book. When he signed for those who had purchased, he would close his eyes, pause for a moment and then open the book. Whatever caught his eye he would write as a quote before signing his name. This is what he wrote in the front of my book:

". . . I looked for my Self, but my self was gone."

It was completely perfect and moved me to tears.

I've only participated in the *Dances of Universal Peace* a few other times after that. When you start out with such a powerful experience, lead by the co-founder of the organization, some of the other experiences tend to pale by comparison.

Reminds me of the first time I ate cheesecake. It was in a London bakery. Hard to top that!

Movement in Nature

For many people, a walk, jog, or hike in nature puts them in a tranquil state that enables them to receive inspiration.

I know several authors who take a walk, with or without their dog, through a meadow or the woods every day. They are writing as they walk. Upon their return, they type everything they contemplated or that came in.

With running or riding a bike, once you get a consistent rhythm going, it is easy to be in a meditative brainwave state. And the endorphins add to the uplifted feeling. The same holds true for horseback riding.

Those who once enjoyed those activities and stop for some reason often feel like something is very wrong, or something is missing. They are not only depriving their body of the healthy benefits of the activity, but they are starving their soul.

Communion with Source is fundamental to a healthy, happy, and fulfilling life.

If people spent half as much time in meditation as they do worrying about things, there would be a lot fewer problems in this world.

Those who have the spiritual gift of writing, music, painting, gardening, or whatever the gift is, absolutely must express those gifts in order to feel whole. A writer must write. A painter must paint. A musician must spend time with his or her music. Otherwise, the life force energy (Chi or Qi) does not flow properly in their body and their life. The expression of their God-given gifts is their prayer and meditation. It is fundamental to happiness.

Walking the
Labyrinth

A Labyrinth is a wonderful meditation tool. Labyrinths come in numerous forms. The most famous is the labyrinth found at Chartres Cathedral in France.

The image is my son, Jess, walking the labyrinth at the St. Francis Basilica in downtown Santa Fe, NM.

My friend, Eve Hogan, author of *Way of the Winding Path: A Map to the Labyrinth of Life*, indicates that "The labyrinth is an ancient path of pilgrimage, rich with meaning."

I've already shared with you how powerful pilgrimage can be.

In a private message, Eve shared the following, "As we simply observe our experience in the labyrinth, we gain valuable insights into our lives and ourselves . .

. As you walk into the labyrinth, the object is to practice self-observation. In my experience, this is one of the most important skills that we can develop. Self-observation brings about awareness. When we are aware of what we are doing and thinking, we realize we have the power to choose differently if what we are thinking or doing are not serving us. When we find our minds wandering as we walk, we can practice focusing on the present moment, on the walk.

When we become aware of what we are experiencing on the labyrinth, we can look at what that represents metaphorically in our lives. For instance, if you are bored on the labyrinth, boredom is probably an issue in your life. If you judge others on the labyrinth, judgment is your issue. If you worry about what people are thinking of you as you walk, your need for approval is your issue. So the labyrinth acts as a sort of microscope shining a light on the areas of our being that may need a little shifting. In addition, it serves as a place to *experience* peacefulness and calm, where we can quiet the busy-ness of our minds and really listen to the whisper of our hearts. We can gain clarity as we walk, receive answers to our questions, let go of stress and discover richer aspects of our being."

Walking the Labyrinth in San Francisco

My first labyrinth experience was an adventure in itself.

I was moving from Pennsylvania to the San Juan Islands of Washington State. It was a powerful journey on many levels. I was leaving the comfort and security of a very high paying job and heading into the unknown to co-found a non-profit for dolphins and whales.

The journey began in Pennsylvania. From there I headed to Virginia to store a few of my things at my parent's home. Then I continued south into the Great Smokey Mountains. I then headed west crossing the entire country. Finally into California where I picked up I-5 and began the long trek north.

I often save articles and bits of information that I think are important. When you are moving and everything you are taking with you is in a little red sports car, you can't take much. I'd only brought with me a few boxes of papers and a few books.

As I neared San Francisco, I remembered that there was a fabulous labyrinth at some church there. I had read an article about it in a magazine several years before.

Was there any chance that I actually had that article with me? I stopped the car to find out.

Unbelievable!

I not only had the article, but it was easily found. Now I knew the name of the church, but I had no idea where it was in the city.

Spending hours getting lost in San Francisco was not my idea of a good time. Did I dare to simply drive in hoping I could find the way or easily get directions? I thought about it for a brief moment and decided to go for it.

As soon as I was across the bridge into the city, I stopped at a gas station to ask for directions. The people there had never heard of the church. (You have to realize that this was 1996, before GPS, cell phones, and high-speed internet were commonplace.)

Again I had to make a decision. Should I simply trust and wander further into the city, or should I head back out, returning to I-5 and the path that I knew?

Luckily I'm a risk taker.

I simply drove while following my instincts. I stopped at a church, but it wasn't the one I was looking for. Again I questioned myself about staying or going? Once again I decided to trust.

Before I knew it, the church was right in front of me. I was completely in awe of how that happened. No directions, no idea of where the church was in the city, and I was able to find it.

After parking the car, I went up to the big doors to the church. I was so excited by now I could hardly contain myself.

When I walked in, I was dumbfounded. The labyrinth on the floor was covered up with folding chairs.

Oh no!

I couldn't believe that I had been so beautifully guided to the church, and now I couldn't walk the labyrinth.

It made no sense. I have never experienced the Universe sending me on a wild goose chase. There is always a point to everything. Even things that look like they are complete detours and sidetracks tend to unfold into something profound in the end. So what the heck was this all about?

I noticed a glass case on the wall with some information posted that talked about the labyrinth's history. Somewhere in there, it mentioned the building of a labyrinth outside.

Thank heavens!

I soon discovered the gorgeous labyrinth behind the church. I was the only one there, so I got to walk the path alone at my own pace in complete silence.

I hadn't read about what you are supposed to "do" while you walk the path. I simply did what felt right. On the way in I was letting go of the things I wanted to leave behind. When I got to the center, I stayed for a few moments and received some new insights. As I walked back out on the same path I took in, I was consciously choosing my future.

It turns out that those are the recommended actions to take while walking a labyrinth path. I simply did them instinctively.

Just as I was finishing my walk, several other people arrived and began their journeys along the path. I had been there precisely at the right time to enjoy walking alone.

I was soon back in my car heading up I-5. The whole detour in and out of San Francisco, including finding the church and walking the labyrinth, took less than two hours.

Enhancing Meditation

"Meditation of the Lord is the highest of the deeds, through which myriads obtain release, through which the thirst (of desires) is quenched, through which one becomes all knowing, through which the fear of death goes away, through which all the desires are fulfilled, through which the dirt of the mind is cleansed and the Nectar of the Name of God is absorbed in the mind." ~ Guru Nanak

Ways to Enhance Your Meditations

There are numerous ways to enhance your meditation experiences. Utilizing these methods will assist you to go to deeper levels of self and higher levels of consciousness. They will allow healing to occur on many more levels and at an accelerated rate.

Fasting

For eons, shamans, monks, sages, and other spiritual beings have practiced fasting in order to attain deeper levels of meditation and prayer.

I don't practice fasting in a formal way. However, I do find that when I am "bringing in" lots of information, I rarely eat until mid-afternoon. It isn't that I am fasting on purpose. It is that I am basically living on Light. The energy sustains me and I feel no hunger.

However, when I am bringing in new energies, I become ravenous. I find that high frequency burns up nutrients extremely fast. So taking a mineral supplement daily and eating heavy foods sometimes is required to sustain my body properly.

Fasting can be a great way to access higher levels of wisdom. Sundance, sweatlodge, vision quest, and other earth-based spirituality rituals are almost always done while fasting. Many religions suggest fasting on occasion.

As with all things that can affect your physical health, I recommend checking with a trained healthcare professional before fasting. There are numerous programs available that involve cleansing teas, herbs, and other nutrient-rich beverages to help you maintain the necessary fluid levels and nutrients you need while not eating solid food.

Silence is Golden!

Silence is a much easier method and extremely effective. Just be in silence for as long as your available time allows. Turn off the tv, radio, music player, video game, phone, and be in silence.

Go out into nature and walk by a stream, sit with your back against a tree, lie on the grass gazing at the clouds or stars. In the next chapter, you will learn how to connect with the elements. Do that alone in silence and I am confident you will reap great rewards.

When I was first "waking up" to spirituality in my early 30's, I was blessed with living alone. In addition to studying meditation, energy healing, channeling, dowsing, metaphysics, and all the rest, I spent countless hours in silence, often in nature.

Many weekends I went home from work on Friday evening, walked in the door, turned off the telephone, and did not emerge to interact with the rest of the world until Monday morning.

If you find that total silence doesn't seem to work for you, then try beautiful uplifting music or recorded nature sounds. As long as no-one is talking or singing words, then your mind does not have to engage to understand what is being said. It is then free to soar to the greatest heights or explore the greatest depths of who you are.

At the 8-day *Warriors in the Mist* training with Stuart Wilde, every time we were in motion, we were to be in silence. That means we were silent and inner-reflecting whenever we walked from one location to the next, rode the ski lift to the top of the mountain for morning and evening teachings, meditations, and tai chi, while blindfolded in a van unaware of where we were being taken, and even while riding horses bareback and blindfolded.

Energy Healing Tools

Energy healing, also called energy medicine, facilitates coming into resonance with health, happiness, inner peace, and gaining an overall sense of wellbeing. Technologies such as flower and gem essences, hands-on healing, crystals, color, sound, and other forms of energy medicine bath the body, and the subtle bodies, with healing frequencies. This, in turn, can raise the person up energetically allowing healing, insight, and accelerated personal growth to occur much more easily.

It also assists in the release of lower, denser frequencies stuck in cellular memory and the emotional body. Until these energetic anchors of trauma and emotional pain from the past can be released, the individual remains stuck, frustrated, and seemingly unable to make progress in the areas of their life in which they wish to improve.

Dancing Dolphin Essences raise you up into such an exquisite place. I created the Dancing Dolphin Roll-On called Meditation specifically to enhance the meditations in *Peering Through the Veil* and to assist you to go deeply within and find the relaxed state necessary for powerful healing meditations.

Group Meditations

A very powerful way to enhance meditation is with a group.

"Where two or more are gathered" is more than just a nice idea. When more than one person is peering through the veil, each person has greater access. It can be done in person, by phone, or when two or more people simply agree to begin meditating at a specific time.

Each year at Spring and Fall Equinox I lead the *Golden Water Dolphin Meditation for Planetary Healing.* It is a guided meditation that I received while in deep meditation. Feel free to join people from all over the world in this lovely healing meditation that you can do from the comfort of your own home:

http://www.dolphinempowerment.com/cetaceanmed.htm

One of my dear friends, Millie Stefani, participated with a group that met each week for an hour to meditate together. They continued this practice for 30 years.

Millie and I meditate together by phone quite often. While in the middle of a conversation, we will find ourselves suddenly in a meditative state. Very quickly one of us is receiving images, feelings, or words. One person is "holding space" which allows the other greater access to Higher Wisdom. We receive meditations, techniques, and answers to personal and planetary questions.

If you participate in a group meditation, make sure that the energy, focus, and feel of the people are in alignment with you.

Finding a meditation facilitator who has the ability to help you access greater wisdom and aspects of self is a gift to yourself. If you participate with a group and you feel that nothing seems to be happening, then going there seems rather pointless.

If you just want social companions, then, by all means, participate in group meditations that are what I call "shallow." But if you are really dedicated to learning, growing and becoming much more than you are now, seek out the ones who can really move energy, where you feel euphoric afterward, where you know something really significant just happened even if you can't describe it in words.

Word of Caution: If you participate in any kind of group, be it meditation or otherwise, and afterward you feel tired, foggy or confused, it is highly likely that something that was said or done (visibly or invisibly) was not beneficial for you. Until you can determine the cause of the confusion, it is best to avoid the people and circumstance.

Grounding Exercise After Meditation

Really powerful group meditations, and sometimes ones you do on your own, can sometimes leave you feeling ungrounded – a bit light headed, dizzy, or spacey. Don't drive under those circumstances.

Some effective ways to "ground" are to

❖ eat something,

❖ do a grounding meditation, or

❖ use the Dancing Dolphin Grounding Essence. It was made with 3 powerful grounding crystals.

A Simple Grounding Meditation

Do this either standing or sitting. Close your eyes. Make sure your feet are flat on the ground or floor. Slowly follow your breath as you breathe in and out, allowing yourself to become calm and centered.

Imagine that you are a tree growing roots out of the bottoms of your feet. Watch the roots move down and branch out deep into the earth. Make the main tap root from each foot as wide as possible. You should feel a shift.

Once you feel more solid, you can open your eyes and go on about your day.

Clearing the Energy Channels

Those who study Transcendental Meditation™, or other eastern forms of meditation, often also practice Yoga.

Sun Salutes, a fluid series of yoga postures, are often done prior to meditation. They help prepare the body to get the most out of the meditational experience. It also lets the body move, stretching and contracting the various muscle groups so that you can more easily remain still while in meditation.

The Sun Salute, Chi Kung, Tai Chi, and other energy movement exercises get the energy moving in your energy body ~ the meridians inside the body, the aura outside the body.

I channel not only information, but Divine frequencies as well. It requires that my body be finely tuned and that the energy channels remain open, the energy centers spinning properly and in harmony with one another. This allows me to radiate energy to those around me, focus it long distance to clients, and infuse it into the energy healing products and tools I create.

Energy healing practitioners who do movements to keep their energy system clear and flowing are often much more effective. It can enhance their ability to work with energy. Chi Kung practitioners do body movements that keep the energy channel clear. That is one of the reasons that Chi Kung is such an effective method of healing. There is a great deal of energy coming through the open channels of the practitioner.

The following pages offer several additional ways to enhance your meditations.

Working with the Elements

O ver the years, I've received many insights through Divine Revelation. They typically happen during, or immediately after, a deep meditation.

One of the insights I received was about meditating with a particular element: earth, air, fire, or water. There are times when you will feel drawn to one more than another. And your particular astrological sign will assist you in choosing the one that is most beneficial for you to start with.

Earth Signs: Capricorn, Taurus, Virgo

Air Signs: Aquarius, Gemini, Libra

Fire Signs: Aries, Leo, Sagittarius

Water Signs: Cancer, Pisces, Scorpio

I classify the sweatlodge as a fire ceremony. Even though it includes all the elements, the level of extreme heat puts it in the fire category for me.

Doing a fire walk or meditating while staring into a flame are also fire meditations. If you feel drawn to fire, then these various methods may offer you great assistance. I often tell people who are a fire sign in astrology to meditate staring at a lit candle or the dance of flames in a fire.

People who are drawn to the earth can gain insight by making pottery, digging in the soil, walking barefooted in nature, or meditating while sitting on the earth or on a large flat stone or boulder. They also might enjoy holding a rock or playing with crystals and gems. Doing a meditation while holding a stone, or placing several on your body, can be a wonderful experience.

Those who align with air often enjoy high places and wind. Wind chimes are very relaxing for them. They might also enjoy watching a bird soaring through the air. I love to do a guided meditation where I imagine becoming the bird soaring ... *what a feeling of freedom.*

Water is my favorite element. I like to hear water over rocks in a stream, or the sound of the surf landing on the shore. I love baths, and my showers are typically extra long as I am being cleansed and receiving information at the same time. I receive great insight when I am in or near water. I love to watch the sun rise or set over the ocean and to meditate near waterfalls.

Try meditating with an element. Or an even better idea is to do four separate meditations, each with a different element. I know you will find one that feels absolutely perfect for you.

Meditation with Crystals

Avery effective way to enhance meditation is with crystals. It works best for those who are sensitive to the subtle frequencies that crystals emit.

Many women love jewelry because of how it makes them feel. I'm not talking about how they might feel rich because they are wearing diamonds, rubies, and sapphires. I'm talking about the uplifted feeling they get by wearing those and other gems.

Every rock, crystal, and gem has its own note (frequency tone) that it sends out.

Well, let's back it up and say that everything in the third-dimensional world is vibrating. We all learned this in science class. Things that appear solid are actually made up of empty space with fast-moving particles being read by our brain as a solid form.

I use the word tone to describe all vibrations including light, because, with the proper instruments or sensitivity, every vibration can actually be heard.

Natural things like rocks, animals, people, and trees have a unique tone they send out as they vibrate. And people who are sensitive to subtle frequencies can see an aura, hear a tone, or feel (sense) a difference.

Man made items like plastic literally feel dead to me.

The more you meditate, spend time in nature, raise your consciousness, and get in touch with the more spiritual side of life, the more highly refined and sensitive you will become to subtle energy.

Every similar group of things has a similar tone. All rose quartz has a vibration that falls within a particular range. Each member of the group has a slightly different tone within the overall group tone. Each unique rose quartz feels a little bit different. It is still obviously rose quartz. But it is a unique rose quartz.

People, for example, have a tone that is different than a dog. The same is true of rose quartz, clear quartz, and what is referred to as spirit quartz. To a scientist, quartz is pretty much quartz. To a metaphysician, however, each one is vastly unique.

Having said all of that, I suggest you go with your gut instinct. Pick them up, hold them in your hand, and see how they make you feel.

Some feel tingly like you can actually feel a pulse or vibration coming from them. Others get very hot. Some stay cold. Some feel good. Others feel like you can't wait to put them down. When you find one you like, that's the one for you.

I can usually spot the crystal or piece of jewelry I want from half way across a room. They seem to call to me even before I reach the table they are on.

One of the best places to find rocks to play with is a lapidary show. They are typically significantly less costly than in a showroom somewhere, and the tone is every bit as pure. It usually doesn't matter if they are tumbled, cut, polished, or in the raw state in which they were found.

It's also fun to learn how to find them yourself. My son has recently become a "rock hound." With the right hammer, a location with particular stones, and the wisdom to know when you've found one, finding your own can be extremely rewarding.

Just like people enjoy different kinds of music, rock lovers enjoy all different types and sizes of stones. They all emit a different tone, and they are all fun to get to know.

I'm only going to mention a few crystals here to get you started. A Google search will quickly bring you hundreds of thousands of websites to visit to learn more about the various stones and their healing properties. I've listed a few book sources in the *Resources* section.

One of the first stones I ever meditated with was Azurite. I was one of nine women taking a nine-month *Women's Wisdom* course through *Heart of the Goddess* near Philadelphia, PA. It was a great class.

We each put an azurite stone on our third eye (middle of the forehead) as we lay on our mat. Azurite is a very deep blue stone. We were taken on a guided meditational journey by one of our instructors. Everything in the meditation was blue: blue sky, blue walls, blue water, etc. At one point we were even guided to swim in the blue water. I found that an extraordinary feeling.

I was hooked on crystals after that.

So, placing a crystal on your third eye is one way to use it in a meditation. You can do that with any stone, gem, or crystal. Try different ones and see what difference they make for your meditations.

I've already described how to make a medicine wheel. Using four to eight of the same type crystal of similar size is a great way to do that. Not only are you making an access portal to higher dimensions, but you are also bathing yourself in the particular vibration of the specific crystal chosen. The three most popular crystals are clear quartz, rose quartz (light pink), and amethyst (various shades of purple).

One of my favorite ways to meditate with a crystal is to simply hold it in my hand. A right-handed person "receives" with the left hand. A left-handed person "receives" with the right hand. Ambidextrous people can send or receive with either hand. So hold the crystal, rock, or gem in your receiving hand, close your eyes, and do your meditation.

I have several crystals that just seem to fit in my hand quite nicely. I often find myself holding one of them, sometimes while meditating and almost always when I work with private clients. A few of the stones I use this way are clear quartz, selenite, spirit quartz (it looks like sugar candy and reminds me of faeries) and a piece of coral I found on a beach in Bimini.

Clearing Crystals

Before working with a crystal, gem, or stone, it needs to be "cleared." Crystals are a lot like computers, they pick up "programs" from the people and location they have been exposed to.

There are several effective methods to clear a stone. Sunlight is the easiest and often the most effective. Another method is to hold them under running water or put them in a mesh bag and place them in a stream for awhile. For soft malleable stones, putting them in salt or burying them in the earth are often recommended.

The only stone I've ever had trouble clearing is Mexican jade. I've been given several pieces over the years and each time the stones have been oozing with negative energy. That's not to say that all Mexican jade has dark, negative, or disharmonious energy. It just means that the ones that came my way were all like that.

I remember one time a group had gathered for a lodge. People often brought gifts. It was always humorous to see what might show up. Once we got a moose skull from Canada. The thing was gigantic and had to be brought in on a truck. Not sure why they thought we needed one of those, but there it was nonetheless.

At this particular gathering, a woman had a gorgeous necklace containing three huge Mexican jade pieces. She took it off from around her neck and came over to me to place it over my head. My son, who was probably only six or seven at the time, came running over, snatched it out of her hand and refused to let her put it on me.

The woman who had this necklace was battling cancer. That necklace was so energetically "icky" that I'm convinced by just removing it from her space, her health most likely began to improve.

Another fun way to work with crystals is in elixir form. Many of my Dancing Dolphin formulas contain crystal and gem essences. The chakra kit, that I co-created with Jonathan Goldman, has a unique crystal for each chakra (main energy center). Each chakra elixir also contains a unique color, sound, aroma, and more.

At the time of publication in early 2012, I have over 80 different crystals and gems in essence form. I use many of those in the various blends I create. Using these products, you are not just receiving the energy of the crystal from your hand or your forehead as in the previous methods. You are literally being bathed in the vibrations of the crystals.

My meditations are always significantly deeper and more insightful when I use one or more *Dancing Dolphin* products beforehand.

What I've offered you here is just a short discussion on a very big topic about vibration and energy healing.

For more information, visit the link to read my article about vibrational healing. Professionals in the field have written me for many years saying it is one of the best descriptions and explanations of vibrational healing they have ever come across.

https://www.MagnificentU.com/Energy

Meditation for Healing, Raising Consciousness, & Achieving Enlightenment

Most people turn to a meditational practice in order to calm the mind, relieve stress, and find inner peace.

That's just the tip of the iceberg in what is possible. In earlier parts of this book, I gave you a tiny glimpse into some of the things that are available.

Through meditation, you can:

❖ Receive energetic upgrades,
❖ Access past life memories,
❖ Experience healing,
❖ Raise your consciousness,
❖ Learn to remote view or astral project,
❖ Gain knowledge through direct revelation, and
❖ Much more.

Healing Meditations

Every meditation can be a healing meditation. Many turn into healing meditations without any conscious effort on your part.

I just closed my eyes and pretended to walk a medicine wheel in my mind one day and dolphins spontaneously showed up and began a healing session.

In Mt. Shasta, as I closed my eyes to do a meditation, Mary showed up and sent me healing energy.

As I work with private clients by phone addressing various issues, I am often "inspired" to lead them through a guided healing meditation. Sometimes they are meditations from one of my programs. Others are completely new in the moment for that particular client.

As I explained in the beginning of the book, you can consciously focus on the future you desire to manifest while in meditation. You can focus on healing as well.

While at the deepest part of your meditation, simply intend that you are healed. See yourself, imagine yourself, perfectly healthy and happy to be alive.

Would you run, jump, or skip if your body was functioning better? Then see yourself doing those things. As always when consciously manifesting, the more senses you get involved in your visualization, the more effective and faster the result.

We talked in the last chapter about crystals having energy. Light and color are also powerful forms of healing. A great way to heal is to imagine a sphere of colored healing light surrounding the area of affliction.

For 15 or so years I needed vision correction. At first, I wore glasses. Eventually, I switched to contacts. I never liked either one. I felt unattractive in glasses and having oily skin, I was constantly trying to keep them from sliding off my nose. Contacts caused eye irritation and I developed a severe allergy to one of the cleansers my optometrist prescribed.

I noticed something very interesting when I became pregnant. I no longer needed glasses. Even after my son was born, for the 2 years that I breastfed him, I didn't need glasses then either.

Unfortunately, very soon after the breastfeeding was over, my vision began to degrade and I started having headaches because of eye strain. I thought about it for awhile and realized that my need for vision correction wasn't due to some malfunction of the eye itself. It was obviously hormonal.

I decided fixing hormones was going to be easy.

Healing with Golden Light

While in meditation, I was "inspired" to see (imagine, feel, and sense) golden spheres of light about the size of softballs in the palms of my hands. I then held my hands up just in front of my eyes and imagined the golden spheres of light completely surrounding and penetrating both eyes. I held my hands in front of my eyes, keeping the visualization going, for five minutes or more.

I did this exercise several additional times over the next few days and soon I had no more headaches and I didn't need glasses. That was over 10 years ago.

Now that I'm over 50, in the last year or two, I'm finding I need reading glasses set at the lowest possible level in order to see numbers in the phone book and tiny words on a map. I think it's time to get out the golden balls of light again.

A few years after healing my eyes with the golden spheres of light, Robert March from Australia sent me his eBook called *Bringers of the Golden Ball*. In it, he talks about *The Oneness Blessing* and how golden spheres of light are used in the program.

I always laugh when things like that happen.

People from all over the world fly to India to study with the golden ball Gurus, and I simply meditated and received the information directly from Higher Wisdom one day. Fun!

That's not to downplay the Oneness program. I know several individuals who facilitate the *Oneness Blessing*. It is a beautiful and very uplifting experience. The golden balls are only a small part of that teaching.

The Cooling Soothing Nature of Mint

When something is inflamed, irritated, or "hot," I recommend seeing it bathed in a light milky mint green. It is a very soothing color and it tones down the heat. Try it while you are in meditation.

Peppermint oil rubbed on the skin (diluted and never on broken or tender skin) or diffused in the air is very good for reducing a fever and cooling down inflammation. So in your meditation with mint, try imagining smelling mint as well.

Another option with light is to simply ask what color would most benefit your body, or the particular part of the body, that is experiencing an imbalance. Whatever color pops in your head, see yourself, or the particular area of the body, bathed in that color light. Hold the visual as long as you can.

I'm such a feeling creature that when I visualize a color, connect with a flower, a dolphin, or even a realm of existence, I feel a different feeling within my body with each one. Surrounding myself with vibrant magenta feels very different than sunshine yellow or soothing mint green. Try it for yourself.

Rainbow Light

A very powerful healing light meditation is to get quiet and centered and begin to visualize yourself bathed in the successive colors of the rainbow. Most people start with red and go up the scale.

You can imagine a column of light coming down from the heavens and shining a beam of red light on and around you. Or, you can see yourself in a giant egg of red colored light. Either one works. Hold that image, feel what it feels like, breathe it in. When red feels complete, then go to orange. Do the same for orange. Follow orange with yellow, then green, blue, indigo (deep midnight blue), and finally purple.

If I'm just working with one color it is usually golden white light.

There are many other color choices and reasons to work with the different ones.

Many people like to call in angels or faeries for healing. Depending on your level of sensitivity, you can definitely feel their presence. Some people are blessed with the ability to see them.

Being in the Universal Flow

I've already shared with you several examples of being in flow with the Universe. Hearing the words, "Go now," and following those instructions resulted in closing a business deal with Jonathan Goldman and meeting my future spouse. Knowing I had to be in Mt. Shasta at a certain time or to file my divorce papers on a specific day lead to extraordinary events in both cases.

When you are in tune with the Universe, life often flows much more easily and gracefully. Suddenly a new checkout line opens and you don't have to wait to make your purchase. A parking space comes available only a few steps from the entrance to your destination. These experiences become the norm, rather than the exception.

You think of a person and the phone rings. It's the person you were thinking about on the other end of the phone. You decide you want a certain item and suddenly you see it in a store or a friend gifts it to you out of the blue.

I can't tell you how many times I've done a guided meditation for the first time and started to see or experience something the guiding voice has not described and then suddenly the person will say to do or see exactly what I have just seen. It's like you are so in tune with the meditation that you have skipped ahead. It's a great affirmation that you are in flow.

Sometimes when I'm guiding clients through guided healing meditations, afterwards they will say that they began seeing what I was about to say before I said it. I know many others who have had this occur. Don't be surprised if this happens for you on occasion.

The more you meditate and learn to follow the subtle signals from within, the more often you will experience phenomena such as these.

Enlightenment

Enlightenment means becoming one with all things. I have had that experience on numerous occasions.

You've already read about the time it happened at a Dances of Universal Peace weekend workshop.

The first time it happened was at an *Alivening Weekend* in New Jersey with Glenn Smyly. We were doing a series of processes known as rebirthing. You lie on your back and forcefully breathe a certain way for an extended period of time. It causes your body to take on a lot more oxygen than normal. It helps you release things stored in cellular memory and it can facilitate breakthroughs. It can also cause your extremities to cramp. My hands contorted and it felt like rigor mortis had set in. It was very painful.

After several sessions of this throughout the weekend, we eventually did one where we were imagining sitting on top of a placid lake while we did the intense breathing. As I visualized the beautiful scenery and felt myself hovering above it in a seated meditation pose, I suddenly became the lake and then the ocean and finally the entire earth. The personality "I" was gone and I was all things. It was a glorious feeling for sure.

This experience is why I was moved to tears when Neil Douglas-Klotz signed his book, ". . . I looked for my self, but my self was gone." It was a reminder of what it feels like to experience enlightenment.

How to Choose the Best Meditation Form for Yourself

I trust that as you have read through *Peering Through the Veil*, you have tried at least a few of the methods of meditation I have described here for you.

If not, it's time to begin exploring meditation through experience rather than just reading about it.

Where should you begin?

There really is no right or wrong starting point. Every meditation form offers benefit. However, for most people, one or two of the methods will feel much more natural to them than the others.

For the highly intuitive individual, the best method will be fairly obvious.

A great way to enhance your intuition, and to find answers if your intuition isn't already finely tuned, is through pendulum dowsing. After meditation, I feel it is the next, most important skill to learn if you wish to:

❖ raise your consciousness,

- ❖ flow with life instead of struggle against it,
- ❖ know the next move the Universe (God, your Higher Self, your soul) wants you to take,
- ❖ discover the most beneficial nutritional supplements for your current needs,
- ❖ learn how beneficial or detrimental a particular product, person, career, or program is for you, and
- ❖ significantly more.

Teaching you how to chart dowse effectively is a topic requiring another book to explain. I have an online program, teach it live, and have a book on the topic. For those who have been trained, I offer the following chart:

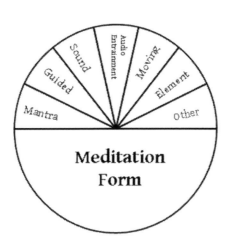

Additional
Meditation Training

T ry the various meditation forms I've given instructions for in this book. Then decide if you'd like to receive training in some of the others. For example, if you try the mantra or yantra meditation and enjoy it, you may want to be trained in Body / Mind, Transcendental Meditation™, or Primordial Sound.

If you do the guided meditation or work with a medicine wheel and find that highly enjoyable, a next step might be to purchase a guided journey audio, seek instruction in Shamanic journey, or the Silva Method™. I created the Magnificent U Meditation Program to accompany this book which contains numerous guided visualization meditations recorded in my voice with beautiful music, ocean sounds, and binaural beats to help your brain gently move into theta.

If you try Tiger Walking or trance dance and want to do more, choose Tai chi, Yoga, or participate in the Dances of Universal Peace.

I hope you have enjoyed *Peering Through the Veil*. In it, I feel I have touched on the most popular forms of meditation. As with

everything in life ... *you are an individual.* Alter and adapt any of the forms until they feel right for you. As I say in my newsletter:

Here's to Your Magnificence!

Epilogue: Your Continued Pursuit of Health, Wholeness, & Happiness

Life is a personal evolutionary journey of ever increasing understanding of truth, expanded awareness, and levels of consciousness. Each successive rise in consciousness from one level to the next requires an even greater, or deeper, level of:

- ❖ forgiveness of self and others,
- ❖ healing of physical, mental, and emotional wounds from the past,
- ❖ letting go of limiting beliefs and fears,
- ❖ open-mindedness,
- ❖ compassion for self and others,
- ❖ letting go of the familiar, comfortable, and commonplace,
- ❖ trust,
- ❖ surrender,

❖ seeking assistance from the unseen (Higher Self, angels, guides, God by whatever name)

The journey is never complete. Meditation is a great tool to assist you along the way. It simultaneously offers assistance to body, mind, and soul.

Meditation is not something you master. It is something you practice. The longer you participate in a meditational practice - days, weeks, months, and years - the greater and more profound the benefits become.

A meditation practice is often a doorway into other areas of personal and spiritual growth. You could be meditating and suddenly have the inspiration to study yoga, visit a new location, call someone you haven't thought about in years, or begin to record your dreams. Often these messages are from your deeper, more enlightened Self ~ what I call the Magnificent Self. Learning to listen to the "still small voice" within can create miracles in your life.

Your limiting beliefs, fears, judgments, and attachment to outcomes cause you to stay stuck at a particular level of consciousness. They are why you experience life the way you do. They are often the reason why you can't seem to get ahead, stay healthy, or be happy for very long.

Becoming aware of those limitations and healing them are how you grow personally and spiritually. It is how you attain higher and higher levels of enlightenment and joy. Many of the tools, techniques, products, and programs that I create are designed to help you heal these issues from the past, learn to flow with whatever the present throws at you, and look to the future from a completely new perspective.

I believe there are 6 practices that assist you in becoming healthy, happy, and whole, body, mind, and soul:

- Meditation – a daily practice of communing with God by whatever name. This helps to still the mind, find inner peace, and receive Divine insights and inspiration. This book is designed to guide you.

- Dowsing – a tool that greatly assists in fine-tuning your intuition, learning to read the subtle hints the universe sends, and letting the Divine Presence know you wish to receive higher wisdom. The pendulums I design and my program *Dowsing for Divine Direction* are available at https://www.Magnificentu.com.
- Spend time alone in silence in nature – to reconnect with the truth of who you are.
- Physical movement practice that opens up the energy centers and flow within the body (Tai Chi / Chi Kung, yoga sun saluations, the Five Tibetan Rites)
- Heal the Disharmony – your physical and emotional traumas of the past, limiting beliefs, fears, and judgments, unrealistic expectations of self and others, attachments to outcomes and how things "should" be.
- Raise Your Vibration – in order to access higher wisdom, experience expanded consciousness, and achieve enlightenment.

My Seed of Divine Restoration and other private long distance energy healing sessions, Dancing Dolphin Alchemical Synergy products, and other programs address healing disharmony and raising your vibration. I trust you will find these products and programs of benefit as you continue your quest for the Magnificent Self.

Get your free audio MP3 here:
https://www.MagnificentU.com/PeeringMP3

If you enjoyed
Peering Through the Veil,
then please give it a positive
review on Amazon
and/or Goodreads!
THANKS!

References

4 Mind 4 Life. "Brain Waves: Health Benefits of Alpha, Theta, & Delta." 4 Mind 4 Life. http://4mind4life.com/blog/2008/08/15/brain-waves-health-benefits-of-alpha-theta-delta/ (January 19, 2011)

Ascension Gateway. "Famous Quotes about Meditation." Ascension Gateway. http://www.ascensiongateway.com/quotes/subject/meditation/index.htm (January 13, 2011)

Ball, Gene. "Keeping Your Prefrontal Cortex Online: Neuroplasticity, Stress and Meditation." The Huffington Post. http:// www.huffingtonpost.com/jeanne-ball/keeping-your-prefrontal-c_b_679290.html (January 13, 2011)

Corder, Mike. "Meditation Guru Who Taught the Beatles." SFGate. http://articles.sfgate.com/2008-02-06/news/17141841_1_roster-of-famous-meditators-interpretations-of-ancient-scripture-medical-respectability (January 13, 2011)

Elevated Existence. "Celebrities Hit the Meditation Mat." Elevated Existence. http://www.elevatedexistence.com/blog/?p=37 (November 6, 2011)

"Famous Quotes About Meditation." Be Inspired and Inspire. http://www.sendwisecards.com/Quotes-about-Meditation.php (January 13, 2011)

Luders, E., Toga, A. W., Lepore, N., & Gaser, C. "The Underlying Anatomical Correlates of Long-Term Meditation: Larger Hippocampal and Frontal Volumes of Gray Matter." Neuroimage, 45(3), 672-678, 2009.

Mayo Clinic Staff. "Meditation: A Simple, Fast Way to Reduce Stress." Mayo Clinic. http://www.mayoclinic.com/health/ meditation/ HQ01070 (July 19, 2011)

McGreevey, Sue. "Eight Weeks To A Better Brain." Harvard Gazette. http://news.harvard.edu/gazette/story/2011/01/eight-weeks-to-a-better-brain/ (March 11, 2012)

Meditation Coach.net. "Meditation the Facts." MeditationCoach.net. http://www.meditationcoach.net/facts.html (January 13, 2011)

MyDeepMeditation.com, "The Intelligence of Soul." The Intelligence of Soul. http://mydeepmeditation.com/contact/ (November 6, 2011)

New Heaven, New Earth. "Food for Thought: Edgar Cayce Sleeping Prophet." New Heaven, New Earth. http://www.nhne.com/ misc/edgarcayce.html (May 8, 2011)

Orsatti, Mario. "Getting Better With Age: Clint Eastwood and Transcendental Meditation." Transcendental Meditation Blog. http://www.tm.org/blog/people/better-with-age-clint-eastwood-transcendental-meditation/ (May 12, 2010)

Stein, Joel. "Just Say Om . . ." Alternative-Doctor.com. http://www. alternative-doctor.com/soul_stuff/just_say_om.htm (January 13, 2011)

"Transcendental Meditation ™." Research Meditation. http://researchmeditation.com/styles/transcendental-meditation-tm (January 13, 2011).

Webb, Ryan. "Meditation for Beginners." Associated Content from Yahoo. http://www.associatedcontent.com/article/2752297/ meditation_for_beginners.html (January 13, 2011)

Wise, Anna. "Awakened Mind Training." Integral Awakened Mind. http://www.3earthfriends.com/sequential-awakened-mind.html (May 2, 2011)

Young, G. Bryan M.D., FRDPC, FRS. "Meditation from Neurological and Rosicrucian Perspectives." The Rose+Croix Journal 2005, Vol. 2. http://www.rosecroixjournal.org/issues/2005/articles/vol2_89_100_young.pdf (May 2, 2011)

List of Figures

Lotus Header Icon, public domain
Candle 01, image by Matthew Green
InnerPeace 1, image by Tosaporn Boonyarangkul
Mantra Mudra, Copyright © 2011 Debbie Shelor
Prayer Mudra, Copyright © 2011 Debbie Shelor
Lotus Light, Copyright © 2010 Debbie Shelor
Portable Buddha Shrine, Copyright © 2011 Debbie Shelor
Mount Shasta 2, image by Mary Ellen Rynes
Digital Drugs Binaural Beats, image by digitalbob8
Dolphin Joy, Copyright © 2010 Debbie Shelor
Bimini Beach, Copyright © 2003 Debbie Shelor
Santa Fe Wheel 01, Copyright © 2003 Debbie Shelor
Santa Fe Wheel 02, Copyright © 2003 Debbie Shelor
Crystal Medicine Wheel, Copyright © 2007 Debbie Shelor
Nambe Sweatlodge, Copyright © 2006 Debbie Shelor
Field of Wildflowers, image by Paul Kempin
Takara with Andi and Jonathan Goldman, image by Mary Britt
Tuning Fork, image by malerapaso
Yoga, image by Michael Lorenzo
Santa Fe Labyrinth, Copyright © 2008 Debbie Shelor
Labyrinth Here?, image by Alan Levine
Crystal Assortment, Copyright © 2010 Debbie Shelor

Resources

Books:

The 7 Secrets of Sound Healing – Jonathan Goldman
Affirmations and other books – Stuart Wilde
The Crystal Bible: A Definitive Guide to Crystals – Judy Hall
The Complete Idiot's Guide to Alchemy – Dennis William Hauck
Creative Visualization – Shakti Gawain
Cunningham's Encyclopedia of Crystal, Gem, and Metal Magic – Scott Cunningham
Dancing with the Wheel - Sun Bear and Wabun Wind.
The Emerald Table: Alchemy of Personal Transformation – Dennis William Hauck
Eyewitness Handbooks Gemstones: The Visual Guide to More than 130 Gemstone Varieties – Cally Hall
Initiation – Elizabeth Heich
The Jesus Code – John Randolph Price
The Life and Teachings of the Masters of the Far East – Baird T. Spalding
Love is in the Earth: A Kaleidoscope of Crystals - Melody
The Macrobiotic Way – Michio Kushi
Manifesting Your Destiny - Wayne Dyer
Shaman, Healer, Sage – Alberto Villoldo
Soul Retrieval - Sandra Ingerman.
Spirit Guides & Angel Guardians: Contact Your Invisible Helpers - Richard Webster
Way of the Shaman - Michael Harner
When the Drummers Were Women - Layne Redmond.

Courses:

Body/Mind Meditation – Greg Schweitzer
The Divine Name –Jonathan Goldman.
Magnificent U Meditation Program – D. Takara Shelor
Manifesting Your Destiny - Wayne Dyer. Nightingale Conant.
Meditation on the Edge - Stuart Wilde.
Shamanic Journey - Foundation for Shamanic Studies - Michael Harner.
The Silva Method™ – Now also available as a home study.
Soul Retrieval - Sandra Ingerman.

Music to Enhance Meditation: (Some of these musical selections include chanting which can enhance meditation if you like listening to it.)

Aeoliah – J'Adore
Chant - The Benedictine Monks
Chakra Chants, Ultimate Om, Holy Harmony, The Lost Cord, Waves of Light, and others – Jonathan Goldman
Crystal Voices - Crystal Voices
Drumbeat or *Rattles* - Foundation for Shamanic Studies.
East of the Full Moon and others - Deuter
Metronome Meditation – Stuart Wilde
Mountain Light - Robert Whitesides-Woo
Music to Walk the Labyrinth, 11:11 Piano Meditations for Awakening, and others - Richard Shulman
Power of the Mantra - Gurumayi
Sacred Earth Drums and others - David & Steve Gordon
The Sky of Mind and others – Ray Lynch
Somewhere in the Silence and others - Donna Michael
The Wave and others - Gabrielle Roth

Index

Takara's Products, Programs, and Energetic Support

Magnificent U Meditation Program

Want to experience the calmness, clarity, inner peace and insight described in this book? Then the Magnificent U Meditation Program is for you! It was designed specifically for those who have enjoyed these teachings and wish to dive deeper in. Each powerful meditation offers a doorway to higher wisdom, healing, insight, a deeper connection to nature and your true essence self, and more. Each audio assists your brain to gently move into a theta brainwave state ... *where deeper healing and transformation are more easily possible.*

Visit https://www.MagnificentU.com/MeditationAudio for more information and to order.

Dancing Dolphin Energy Products

To feel as fabulous and peaceful as you do in your deepest, most beneficial meditations, use *Dancing Dolphin Alchemical Synergy Energy Healing Products.* Dancing Dolphin contains delicately fine-tuned frequencies designed to help you attain and maintain a particular state of BEing. Why wait for years of deep meditation to take effect so you can feel balanced, calm, and peaceful most of the time, when *Dancing Dolphin* products can assist you right now.

Dancing Dolphin products are a synergistic alchemically-combined form of energy healing. Each roll-on, elixir, and mist is lovingly prepared by hand and personally infused by Takara. The result is a completely unique, highly effective, convenient, and affordable method of being raised up in vibration and finding harmonic resonance with your Divine perfection.

https://www.MagnificentU.com/store/

Custom Blends

In addition to the numerous powerful *Dancing Dolphin* oils & mists you can choose from, Takara can create a Custom Blend formulated specifically for you or a group you are leading. She tunes in to your higher self and guides and is "given" the perfect formula to energetically assist you right now with whatever you are facing physically, mentally / emotionally, or spiritually / energetically.

https://www.MagnificentU/Custom

The Essence of Sound Healing with Jonathan Goldman

Using a proprietary process developed by Takara, Jonathan Goldman's powerful sound healing music has been successfully infused into energetic elixirs for you to enjoy. Experience healing sound like never before. It's an experience to delight the senses, a vibration to ignite the Soul.

https://www.MagnificentU.com/Sound

Long Distance Energy Healing Sessions:

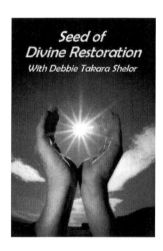

Takara offers Seed of Divine Restoration and private phone consultations for those who desire her personal assistance. The Seed of Divine Restoration is a unique form of healing that Takara received during meditation. The Seed of Light that she gives you during this session sends wave upon wave of healing energy to all aspects of yourself and your life.

https://www.MagnificentU.com/Seed

Here's to Your Magnificence!

Sign up for Takara's free online monthly magazine, Here's to Your Magnificence, enjoyed by thousands of readers from over 100 countries across the globe. Each issue features new articles and insights from Takara, as well as product and program updates and much more. Get a free ebooks or audio when you join the list.

https://www.MagnificentU.com

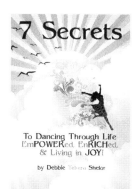

Visit Takara's website to get a free ebook– the *7 Secrets to Dancing Through Life EmPOWERed, EnRICHed, and Living in JOY! (plus several other gifts!)*

https://www.MagnificentU.com/gift/

Comments:

"Takara's Essences of Sound are outstanding. We've used them in large groups of people and they really seem to assist in the frequency shifting experience, adding even more vitality and loving energy to the consciously encoded sounds we either listen to or create." - *Jonathan Goldman, Internationally renowned pioneer in Sound Healing*

"I love the Violet Flame Mist." – *Patricia Diane Cota-Robles, President of the New Age Study of Humanity's Purpose*

"Takara, I want to thank you for the Seed of Divine Restoration . . . After many weeks and incredible lessons, clarity and understanding, I know without a doubt that what I've experienced was from your session and it continues today! Again, THANK YOU. - *Laura K. Redondo Beach, CA*

"We recently began carrying Dancing Dolphin Products (at our store) and I can tell you as a Holistic Health Practitioner & Facilitator, Takara's Essences are a beautiful combination of sacred ingredients and her own form of energy work to promote healing and growth. I have seen the essences help cleanse and center the mind and purify the spirit and aura. As an energy worker, I find these tools to be essential to help clients feel empowered in their own healing process. In fact, I believe in her line of products so much that I use them myself! Even just sometimes smelling the essences or holding them can be enough to open the mind and body to healing and when rolled on, they can have an even longer lasting effect. We all have that sacred journey that we must go on in life and I am proud to say that I am definitely taking her essences along with me!" - *Rev. Andrea Teague, SPD, Life & Spiritual Life Coach, Massage & Bodywork Practitioner*

182

About the Author

Debbie "Takara" Shelor is a bestselling author, award-winning speaker, engineer, and mystic. People the world over affectionately refer to her as Takara ... *a name she received in meditation.* She later discovered that it means treasure and blessing in Japanese.

Her first life-altering mystical encounter happened at the tender age of 14.

She discovered in her late 20's how profound a radical shift in diet and the addition of powerful herbal supplements could be in overcoming the health issues she had been challenged with most of her life.

At the age of 33, while working as an Industrial Engineer and front line supervisor in the pharmaceutical industry, she underwent another radical shift. Job-related stress caused a deeply buried emotional trauma to surface and she experienced what some would term a complete emotional meltdown.

This dark night of the soul caused her to seek ways to heal the emotional pain. She studied, and began to apply, numerous techniques, including meditation. Dolphins suddenly began appearing every time she meditated. Their presence was always accompanied by the same exquisite Divine Feminine healing energy she had experienced in her teens.

That launched a 20+ year exploration of an extraordinary array of meditation techniques, energy healing methods, and pathways to enlightenment.

She has been illuminating the way for others for over 2 decades through books, articles, newsletters, private consultations, and workshops. Her online magazine, *Here's to Your Magnificence*, has thousands of subscribers from over 100 countries across the globe.

Her mystical connection and daily practice of meditation have opened gateways to higher levels of wisdom, healing, and consciousness. She shares these Divine gifts through her writing, the various products she creates, the long distance energy healing transmissions she offers, and by leading transformational workshops on-line, on land, and at sea.

Her *Dancing Dolphin Energy Healing Products* have been thrilling customers the world over since 1998. Part of the Dancing Dolphin product line includes the *Essence of Sound*, co-created with sound healing expert, Jonathan Goldman.

She is the owner of *Forchianna L.L.C.*, creator and primary instructor for *Magnificent U*, and co-founder of *Joy Weavers International.*

> "How do you thank someone who comes into your life and because of her influence your life is changed forever? Takara has graced my life with her many talents and skills. Especially through her healing arts, I have made quantum leaps forward in my life. At one crisis point, she was able to facilitate my integration of a significant shift in only 10 minutes! I had been beside myself for 2 weeks. Her knowledge and keen ability to share it have enriched my life forever! Perhaps due to her

engineering and teaching background she has an amazing ability to take extremely complex concepts and information and boil it down to bottom line usefulness with clarity. She makes things implicitly simple and understandable to a lay person. Her extensive studies in metaphysical and philosophical areas allow her to create freeways for those of us who don't have time to sift it all out. The clarity she creates with her accelerated techniques allows you to quickly come on-line with the information, to transition, and to push past limitations."

- Theresa Wright, Carlsbad, CA

Visit her online at: https://www.MagnificentU.com. Get one of her eBooks for free when you sign up to receive her monthly newsletter, *Here's to Your Magnificence!*

Printed in Great Britain
by Amazon